Best Editorial Cartoons of the Year

BEST EDITORIAL CARTOONS OF THE YEAR

1979 EDITION

Edited by
CHARLES BROOKS

Foreword by **JERRY ROBINSON**

Gretna 2001

Copyright © 1979
By Charles G. Brooks
All rights reserved
ISBN: 0-88289-229-0, Hardcover
ISBN: 0-88289-230-4, Paperback

Special acknowledgments are made to the following for permission to use copyrighted material in this volume:

Editorial cartoons by Lou Grant, © Los Angeles Times Syndicate; by Jeff MacNelly, © Chicago Tribune–New York News Syndicate; by Dick Wallmeyer, © Register and Tribune Syndicate; by Frank Interlandi, © Los Angeles Times Syndicate; by Jim Berry, © Newspaper Enterprise Association, Inc.; by Hugh Haynie, © Los Angeles Times Syndicate; by Jack Bender, © Rothco; by Jim Lange, © The Daily Oklahoman; by Jimmy Margulies, © Rothco; by Ed Valtman, © Rothco; by Art Henrickson, © Paddock Publications; by Jerry Robinson, © Cartoonists and Writers Syndicate; by Dwane Powell, © The News and Observer Publishing Co.; by Francis Brennan, © Newsweek; by Eldon Pletcher, © Rothco; by Doug Sneyd, © Sneyd Syndicate; by Mike Konopacki, © Rothco; by David Levine, © NYREV, Inc.; by Dave Granlund, © Newspaper Enterprise Association, Inc.; by Draper Hill, © The Detroit News, distributed by King Features Syndicate; by Mark Taylor, © Rothco; and by Steve Greenberg, © Van Nuys Publishing Co.

In the event any necessary permissions for the use of copyrighted material have been omitted through error, acknowledgments and apologies will be made.

Library of Congress Serial Catalog Data

Best editorial cartoons. 1972-
   Gretna [La.] Pelican Pub. Co.
   v. 29cm. annual-
"A pictorial history of the year."

   I. United States—Politics and government—1969—Caricatures and Cartoons—Periodicals.
E839.5.B45   320.9'73'09240207   73-643645
ISSN 0091-2220   MARC-S

Manufactured in the United States of America
Published by Pelican Publishing Company, Inc.
1000 Burmaster Street, Gretna, Louisiana 70053

Contents

Foreword	6
Award-Winning Cartoons	11
Carter Administration	17
Camp David—Mideast	32
Politics	45
America's Economy	49
The U.S. Dollar	55
Foreign Affairs	67
Supreme Court Rulings	72
Koreagate	77
The U.S. Congress	81
The Soviet Union	89
U.S. Defense	97
Taxpayers' Revolt	101
Richard Nixon	108
Africa	111
Energy	115
Crime	120
The Postal Service	123
South of the Border	126
Test Tube Baby	131
Equal Rights Amendment	135
Canada	137
The Environment	141
Choosing a Pope	145
Obituaries	147
... And Other Issues	151
Past Award Winners	157
Index	159

Foreword

THE ART OF THE POLITICAL CARTOON

"The man who cannot visualize a horse galloping on a tomato is an idiot," wrote Andre Breton, the French poet regarded as the founder of Surrealism, the literary and visual arts movement. The editorial cartoon can be regarded in great measure as Surrealistic art. The potent effect discovered by Surrealists of two or more disparate elements on a plane alien to both has been employed by the political cartoonist and the Surrealist painter. The unexpected association of images of Surrealist art—as well as the political cartoon—frequently has all the strangeness of a dream. The floating figures in David Low's "The Angels of Peace Descend on Belgium" (1940) have the same dreamlike and magical qualities found in Marc Chagall's "Flying Over the Town" (1914). While Chagall's Surreal figures are romantic and joyous, Low's flying troupe of Himmler and his Gestapo aides executing a dance of death evokes a frightening nightmare.

David Low: *The Angels of Peace Descend on Belgium* (1940).

Since the creation of the cartoon of political and social satire, there has been a continuous interplay between it and the fine arts. To ignore one is to not fully understand or appreciate the other. The political cartoon is an artistic expression in the "fine arts" tradition, with clear lineage in such movements as Symbolism and Romanticism, as well as Surrealism. Moreover, the political cartoon is often a fusion of graphic art forms *and* literature. Its visual/verbal elements make it a medium of enormous power that reflects the deep cultural absorption of its imagery.

FOREWORD

The relationship of animal and man has been a persistent theme throughout history, from prehistoric cave drawings to the most sophisticated forms of 20th century art. In the Trois Freres cave in France, dating to the Ice Age, there is a dancing human figure with antlers, a horse's head, and bears' claws. Visual representations of animals in ancient civilizations were primarily magical and religious in nature, as in the ancient Egyptian depiction of their gods in animal form. The Egyptians made extensive use of burlesque and caricature as well, and were perhaps the first to picture animals to ridicule man. One artifact shows a lion seated on the king's throne receiving offerings from a goose and a fox representing the high priests.

19th Century French poster: The Millionaire Peacock.

The animal proved to be a continuing motif in man's graphic expression. Aristotle codified the belief that to read the character of a man, one could but trace in his physiognomy the features of the animal he most resembled. In 1601 Giovanni Torta first published the theory, later embellished by Lavater in 1775. Francisco Goya used animals to present savage allegories of human behavior and political outrages, as in his portrayal of the presumptuous ass prescribing for a sick man representing Spain. Pablo Picasso's etching, "Minotauromachy" (1935), a marvelous work of modern fantastic art, makes symbolic use of creatures part animal and part human.

The political cartoonist has made perhaps the most fertile use of animal symbology, often to devastating effect. A good caricature is only fully appreciated by those who have been its victims. A case in point was Governor Samuel Pennypacker of Pennsylvania who, after being caricatured as a parrot by Charles Nelan, attempted to pass a law prohibiting "the depicting of men .... as birds or animals." Cartoonist Walt McDougal then drew all the State's top officials as inhuman objects, ridiculing the bill to death. Another classic example is Thomas Nast's unforgettable cartoon entitled "Let Us Prey" in which he depicts Boss Tweed and his gang as vultures perched on a craggy cliff. It was one of the series that sent Tweed into exile and, ultimately, to jail. It was Nast, of course, who created the modern political mythology of the Tammany tiger and the Republican elephant. Among the many other animal symbols employed by the cartoonist have been the Democratic donkey, the Russian bear, and the English lion.

Bernini: Caricature of a Cardinal.

Caricature, a primary tool in the repertoire of the political cartoonist, also had its beginning in animal imagery. At the time of Aristotle, *caricare* meant to change selected features to bring out the latent animal whose nature shaped the man. Sir Thomas Browne wrote in the 17th century that "when men's faces are drawn with resemblance to some other animal, the Italians call it, to be drawn in caricature." Caricature has held a fascination for fine artists as well; from Leonardo da Vinci, Giovanni Bernini, and Pier Leone Ghezzi to Goya, Toulouse-Lautrec, and Picasso.

Leonardo Da Vinci: Caricature, *Ugly Old Woman.*

When caricature was introduced into political prints in the 18th cen-

FOREWORD

tury, it was given a new function. As noted art scholar E. H. Gombrich pointed out, transforming caricature from a studio joke into a social and political weapon to "kill" the powerful and pretentious by ridicule marked a conquest of a new dimension of freedom of the human mind. Emerson once noted, "Caricatures can reveal the essence of a person more accurately than a photograph." Honore Daumier was jailed in 1882 for his devastating cartoons of King Louis Philippe, Charles Phillipon was also rewarded with prosecution by the king, whose features he transformed into a pear. Ernst Kris wrote in *Psychoanalytic Explorations in Art* that the simplifications in caricature gave its own meaning as if that is all the man consists of.

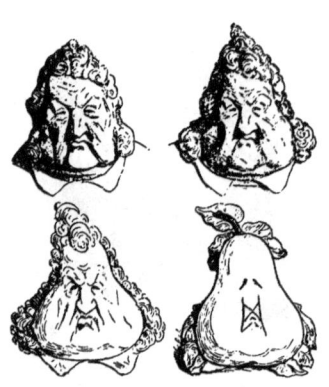

Charles Phillipon: King Louis Philippe and the pear.

Andre Gill popularized the style of large heads on midget bodies (Daumier had used the device in the drawing of Louis Napoleon in his series, *Representents Representes*), and Caran D'Ache and Olaf Gulbransson replaced the chiaroscuro tradition with the precise linear drawing in the late 19th century. By then, caricature in the political cartoon was firmly established in the contemporary journals.

The many symbolic motifs developed by the editorial cartoonist are analogous to the iconography employed by such painters as Stuart Davis, Joan Miro, and Paul Klee. Employing art as a vehicle to advance political, moral, religious, or psychological purpose also had its direct parallel in the editorial cartoon. The cartoon as an instrument of political and social satire, such as Daumier's "The Legislative Body," George Grosz's "Ecce Homo," and William Gropper's "The Senate," has its counterpart, too, in the fine arts, as found in Picasso's "Guernica," Diego Rivera's "Night of the Rich and Night of the Poor," and Jack Levine's "The Feast of Pure Reason." The cross-fertilization of the arts is seen in the many American easel painters who found the political cartoon a rich medium of expression, among them John Sloan, George Luks, Reginald Marsh, and Ben Shahn.

The modern political cartoon is an art of variegated ancestry. It had its beginnings in the social satire of the early 19th century when virtually the only pictorial record of current events were satirical prints, exemplified by the work of William Hogarth, Thomas Rowlandson, and James Gillray. Satirical journals and magazines of caricature flourished in the early 19th century. The political and social cartoon was absorbed into the fabric of the new mass publications such as *La Caricature* (1830), *Charivari* (1838), *Punch* (1841), *Le Rire* (1894), and *Simplicissimus* (1896), featuring the artistry of Daumier, John Leech, John Tenniel, George du Maurier, Toulouse-Lautrec, Max Beerbohm, and Aubrey Beardsley. The graphic weekly came to America, and by the end of the century such magazines as *Puck, Judge* (both in 1881), and *Life* (1883) gave birth to a new age in American graphic, political, and social satire. By the early 1900s the political cartoon had become a permanent fixture in American journalism. With a newspaper in every major American city, it became a powerful force in local, state, and national politics.

James Gilray: John Bull and his family (1792).

Unfortunately, the political cartoon as an art form suffered neglect almost commensurate with its rising popularity. The art establishment has been habitually slow to recognize the cartoon in all its forms as "art." Even Hogarth's satirical works were regarded with horror by contemporary painters while enthusiastically received by the English public. Critic Ignatius Mattingly pointed out, "It may almost be set down as a law of cultural history that the vulgar amusements of today are the high brow art of tomorrow." Italian opera, Elizabethan drama, jazz, and the film were conceived for the entertainment of the masses. It remained for succeeding generations in each instance to detect in them lasting values and form an appreciation of their art. The same has been true of the political cartoon.

This attitude of the art establishment reflects many traditional views of the cartoon in general, and of the political cartoon in particular. A misconception by some critics has been that if a work is humorous or funny, it can't be true art; art, after all, is serious. There is nothing more serious, in fact, as cartoonists well know, than humor. Such attitudes are not unique in art history. Academicians once condemned Caravaggio's paintings as "vulgar," and charged him with destroying "good taste." It was not until the European intellectual extolled the comic strip that Americans took a new look at that unique genre and recognized it as an indigenous American art form. The purists who believe "les beaux arts" should be non-functional dismiss the political cartoon as mere propaganda. Others feel that "true art" deals only in the abstract with grand issues such as war and peace, life and death, and greed and pestilence.

FOREWORD

They think that any work devoted to specific issues which are the usual concern of political cartoons renders that work, ipso facto, beyond the pale of fine art. Traditional dogma, too, dictates that if a work is too popular, it certainly cannot be "art," a notion persisting perhaps from the time when only the well born were educated and possessed the refinement needed for art appreciation.

The political cartoon, like fine art (and unlike such collaborative art forms as the theatre or film), is the creation of an individual that gives it a singular effectiveness. However, unlike the painter (or novelist) whose work is produced over a relatively long period and in stages of refinement lasting weeks, months, or even years, the daily political cartoon is usually conceived and executed in one burst of creativity, within a space of hours. It is then seen by the public within a few days of its conception, endowing it with a spirit of spontaneity and a quality of immediacy unequalled in the arts.

If it is true, as Herbert Read concluded, that "Art is an essential instrument in the development of human consciousness," then the political cartoon has been an essential instrument in man's political and social awareness, and has the same binding and energizing force. As in all genres, the worthiness of the individual cartoon as art depends on the power of the artist. Saul Steinberg and David Levine are among the few cartoonists recognized by the fine art community and exhibited in such museums as the Whitney in New York and the Hirshhorn in Washington, D. C. There remain, however, many brilliant political cartoonists working under the severe pressure of a daily deadline, who have yet to be fully appreciated as artists first.

The political cartoonist is a curious breed. He is at once an artist, social critic, and political analyst. He has the ability to reduce a complex issue to its essentials, both in thought and graphics. He is more sensitive to stupidity than most, and has an instinctive feeling and passion for universal human values. He has an acute sense of the ridiculous; he sees humor in tragedy, and tragedy in humor. Pomposity, social pretensions, sacred cows, and illusions animate his spirit of revenge. What was once written about Blake could also be said of the political cartoonist at his best: "Passion and humor are mixed in his writing like mist and light—whom the light may scorch or the mist confuse, it is not his part to consider."

JERRY ROBINSON

Award-Winning Cartoons

1978 PULITZER PRIZE

JEFF MACNELLY
Editorial Cartoonist
Richmond News Leader

Born in New York City, 1947; grew up in Cedarhurst, New York; graduate of Phillips Academy; attended University of North Carolina; staff artist and editorial cartoonist for *The Chapel Hill Weekly*; joined *Richmond News Leader*, 1970; won Pulitzer Prize for editorial cartooning, 1972, 1978; winner of the first Thomas Nast Award, 1978; honored with George Polk Award, National Cartoonist's Society Award, 1978; syndicated in approximately 400 newspapers by the Chicago Tribune—New York News Syndicate; his comic strip "'SHOE" is distributed to more than 450 newspapers.

1978 THOMAS NAST AWARD

JEFF MACNELLY
Editorial Cartoonist
Richmond News Leader

1977 NATIONAL NEWSPAPER AWARD/CANADA
(Selected in 1978)

**TERRY MOSHER
(AISLIN)**
Editorial Cartoonist
Montreal Gazette

Born in Ottawa, Ontario, 1942; attended Central Technical School, Toronto, 1961-63, Ontario College of Art, Toronto, 1963-64, L'Ecole des Beaux-Arts, 1965-66; free lance cartooning, 1968; staff cartoonist for the *Montreal Star*, 1969-71; art director of *Take One Magazine*, 1969-71; founding and associate editor of *Last Post Magazine*, 1970 to present; staff cartoonist for the *Montreal Gazette*, 1972 to present; taught animation and life drawing at Montreal Museum School of Fine Arts, 1973-74; recipient of Canada Council Grant to study historical and contemporary cartooning and caricature throughout Europe, 1971; cartoons are syndicated throughout Canada by the Toronto Star Syndicate; works under the pen name "Aislin," his eldest daughter's name.

Best Editorial Cartoons of the Year

DAVID LEVINE
Courtesy David Levine

COPYRIGHT © 1978 NYREV, INC.

Carter Administration

As 1978 wore on, more and more Americans were becoming disenchanted with President Jimmy Carter. The reasons were varied. His policies had failed to halt, or even slow, Russian and Cuban intervention in Africa. The dollar—long in trouble—continued its slide, the inflation rate climbed, and Carter's domestic policies seemed to be flops.

The longest coal strike in history—3 months and 18 days—undermined the economy and fanned inflation, and the president seemed powerless to act.

Many Democratic office-seekers expressed reluctance to have Carter come into their states, apparently concluding that his presence would hurt their candidacies more than it would help. After the tentative success of the Camp David peace talks, however, the president's popularity regained momentum, which was clearly reflected in the polls.

Carter ended the year with another big feather in his cap. He had pushed strongly for streamlining government and overhauling civil service. Although not achieving everything he wanted, he was able to get these two important projects through Congress. The former program, however, still had a long way to go.

"Do you take credit cards?"

TOM CURTIS
Courtesy Milwaukee Sentinel

JOHN PIEROTTI
Courtesy Atlantic City Press

"I DON'T KNOW ABOUT YOU, BUT I DID FINE"

"Give it to me straight — do I look besieged?"

JOHN BRANCH
Courtesy Chapel Hill News

KEN ALEXANDER
Courtesy San Francisco Examiner

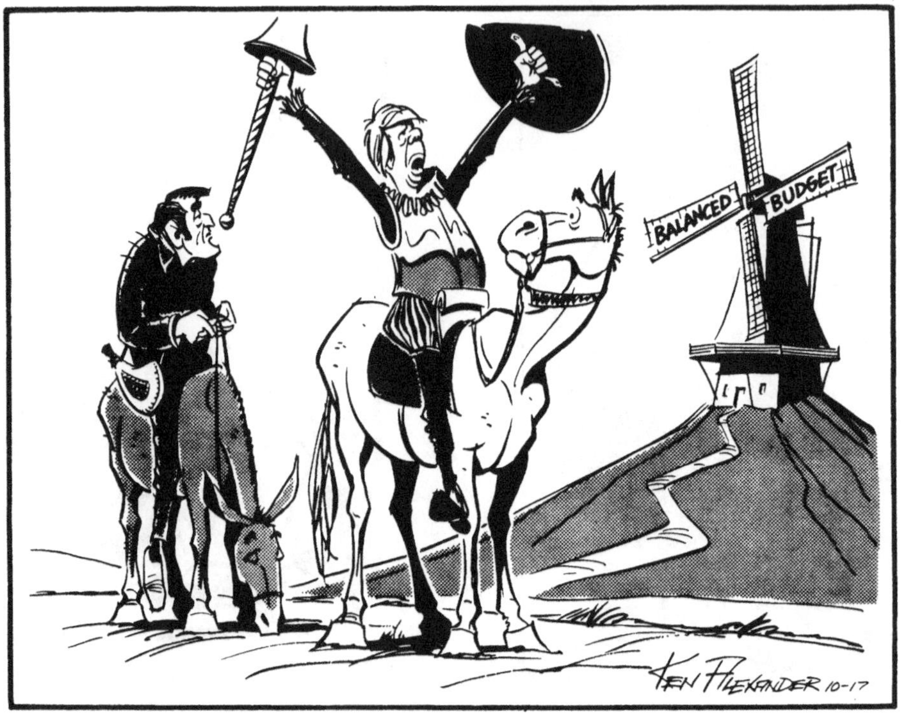
BALANCED
BUDGET
KEN ALEXANDER 10-17

"To Dre-e-e-eam the impossible dre-e-e-eam..."

DICK LOCHER
Courtesy Chicago Tribune

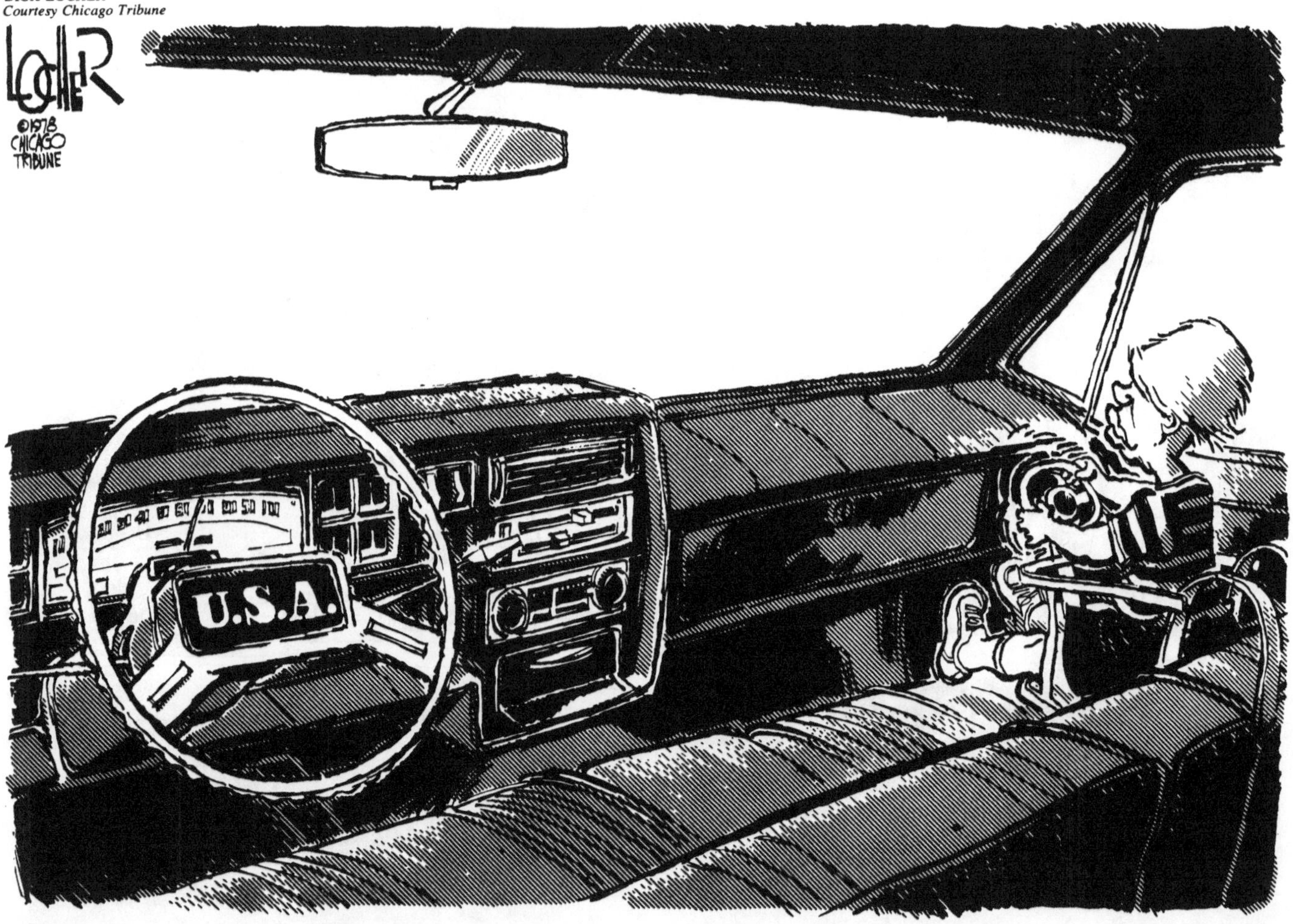
LOCHER
©1978 CHICAGO TRIBUNE
U.S.A.

NOT SCARING ANYONE

EDDIE GERMANO
Courtesy Brockton Daily Enterprise

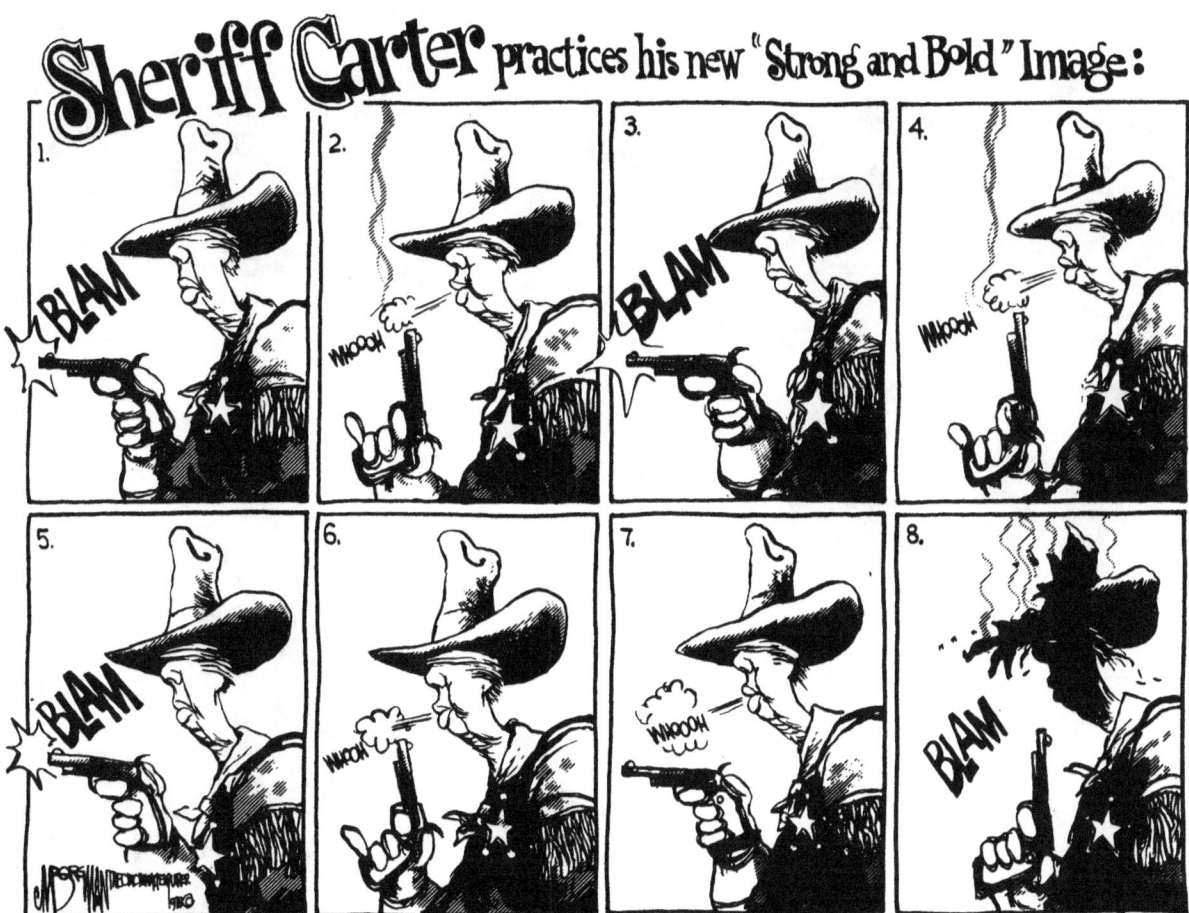

JIM BORGMAN
Courtesy Cincinnati Enquirer

JON KENNEDY
Courtesy Arkansas Democrat

97-pound weakling?

ART BIMROSE
Courtesy Portland Oregonian

CHARLES WERNER
Courtesy Indianapolis Star

STROKE!

FRANK EVERS
Courtesy N. Y. Daily News

CLYDE PETERSON
Courtesy Houston Chronicle

'Yassuh! That's what's been holdin' this 'ministration back! Packin' too much weight!'

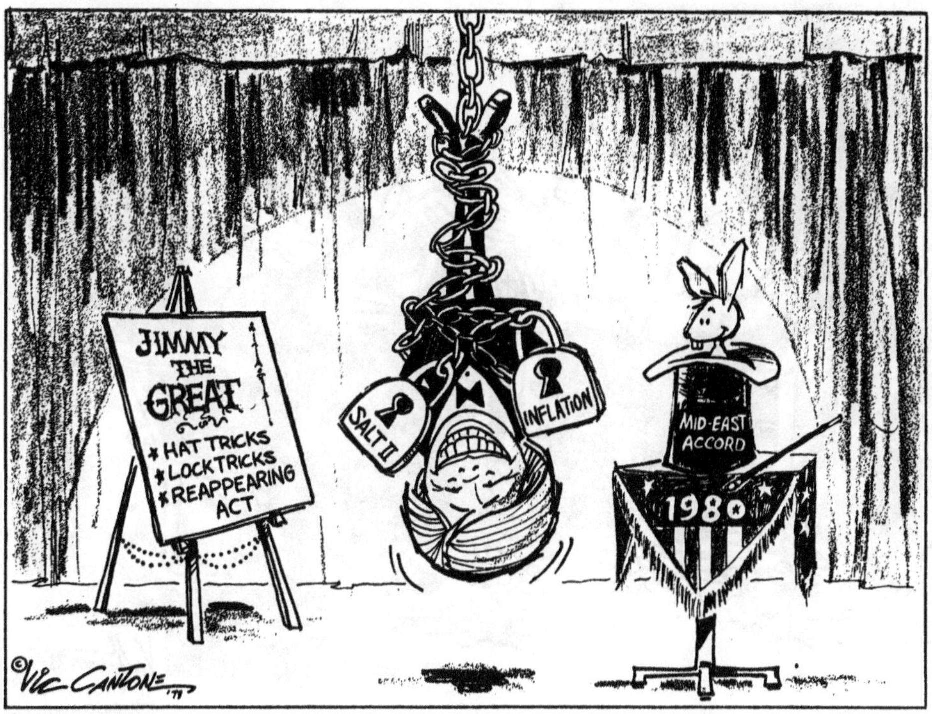
JIMMY THE GREAT
* HAT TRICKS
* LOCKTRICKS
* REAPPEARING ACT
SALT II
INFLATION
MID-EAST ACCORD
1980
©VIC CANTONE '79

VIC CANTONE
Courtesy N.Y. Daily News

..AND FOR MY NEXT TRICK, FOLKS...

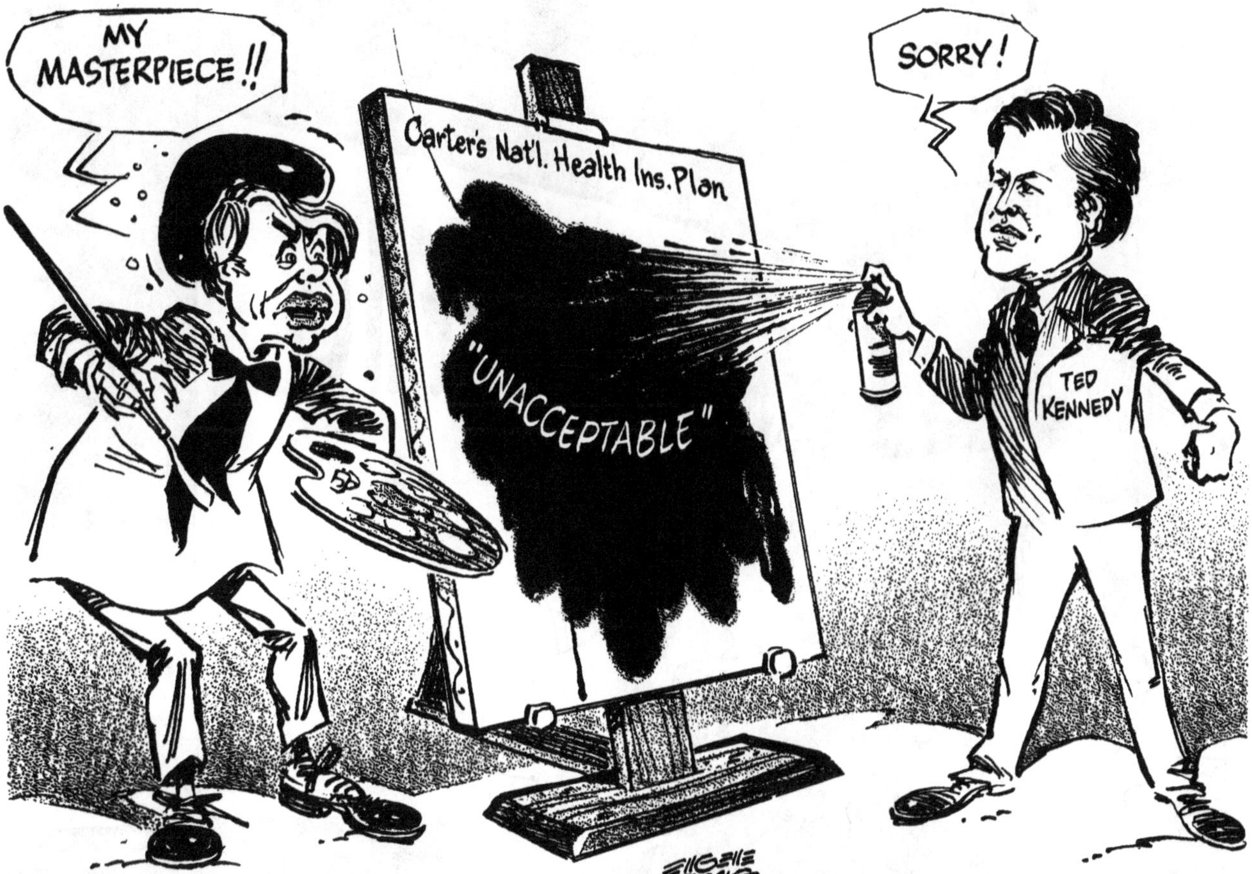
MY MASTERPIECE!!
SORRY!
Carter's Nat'l. Health Ins. Plan
"UNACCEPTABLE"
TED KENNEDY
EUGENE CRAIG

EUGENE CRAIG
Courtesy Columbus (O.) Dispatch

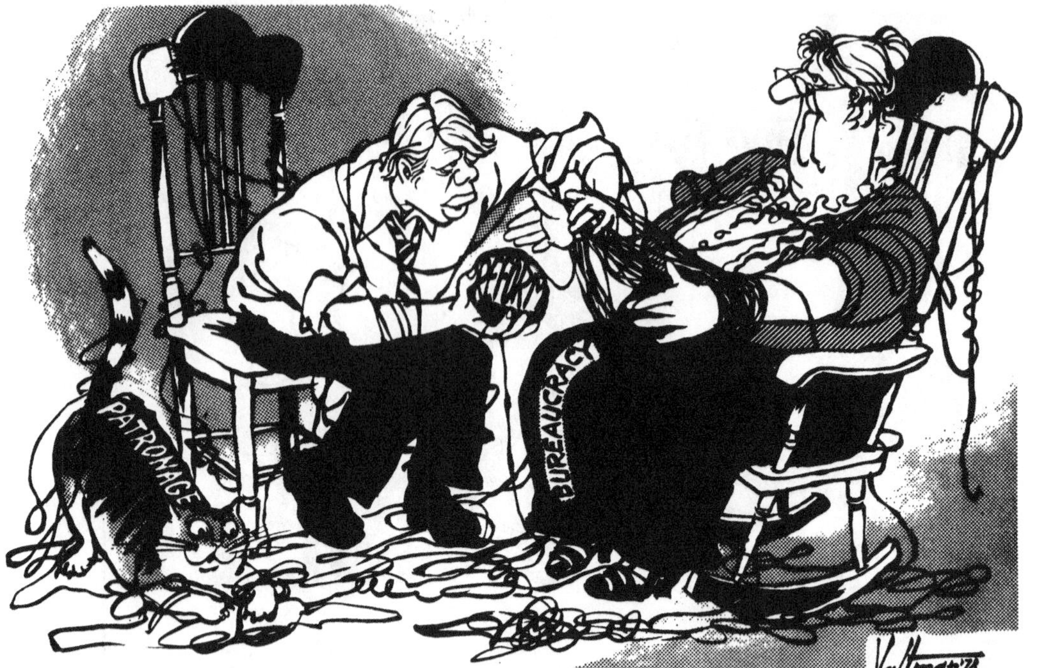
PATRONAGE
BUREAUCRACY
Valtman '78

ED VALTMAN
©Rothco

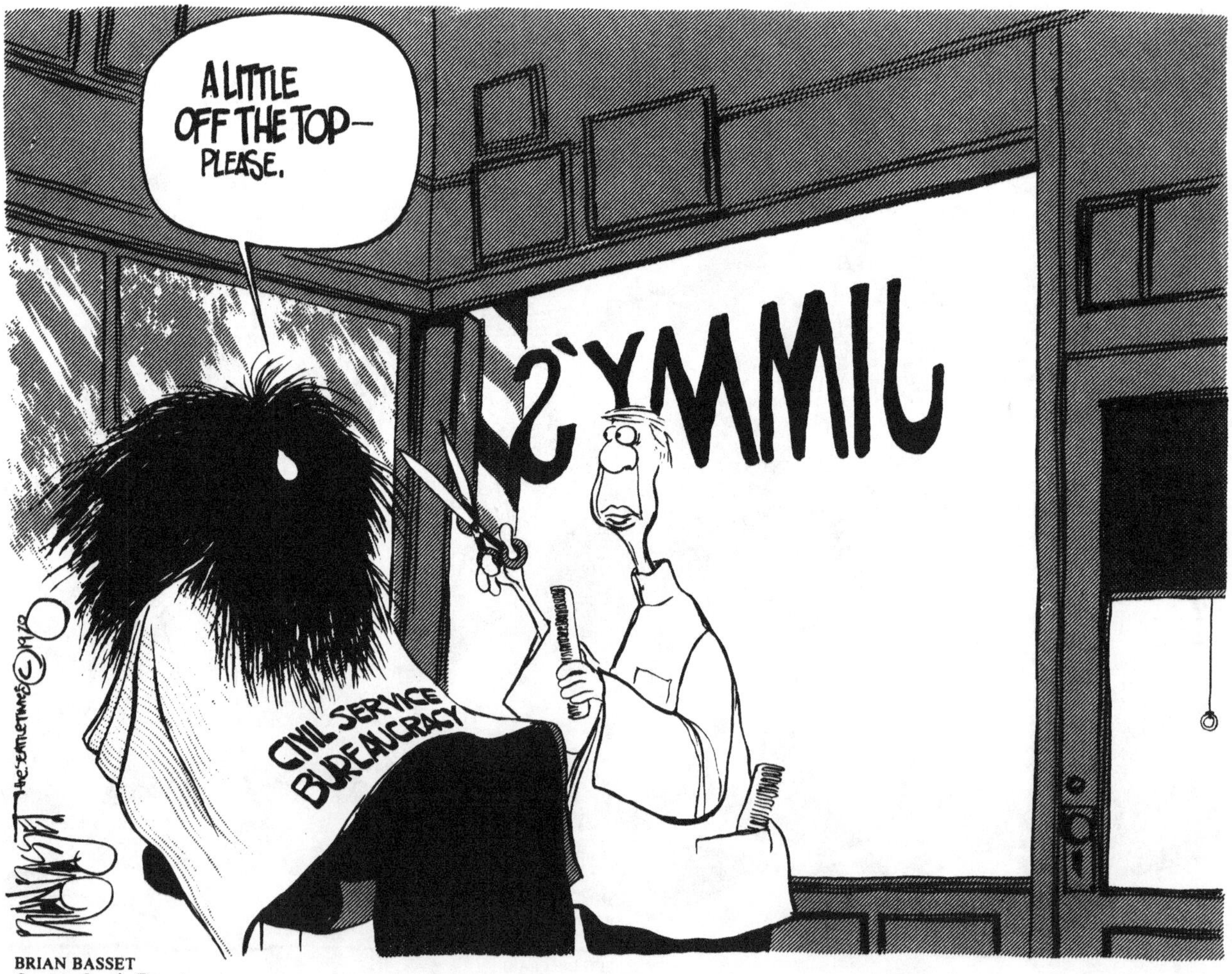
A LITTLE
OFF THE TOP-
PLEASE.
JIMMY'S
CIVIL SERVICE
BUREAUCRACY

BRIAN BASSET
Courtesy Seattle Times

CHARLES BROOKS
Courtesy Birmingham (Ala.) News

BALDY
Courtesy Atlanta Constitution

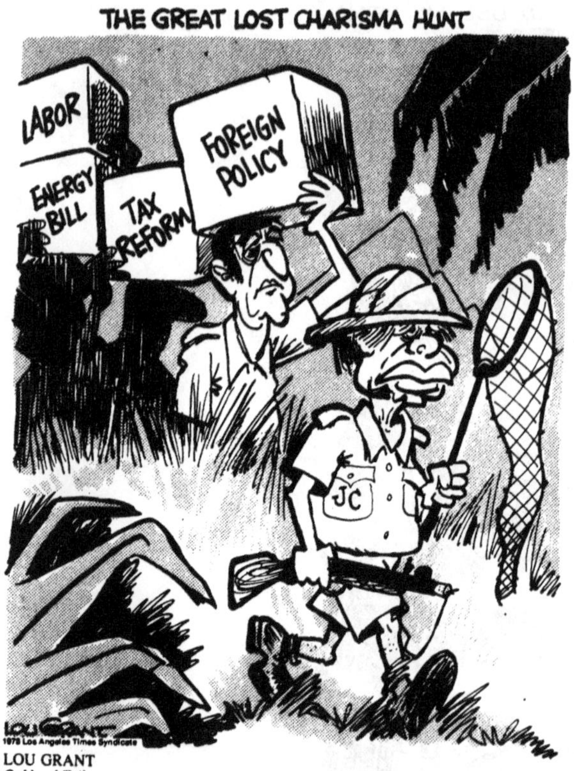
THE GREAT LOST CHARISMA HUNT
LABOR
ENERGY BILL
TAX REFORM
FOREIGN POLICY
JC
LOU GRANT

LOU GRANT
Oakland Tribune
©Los Angeles Times Syndicate

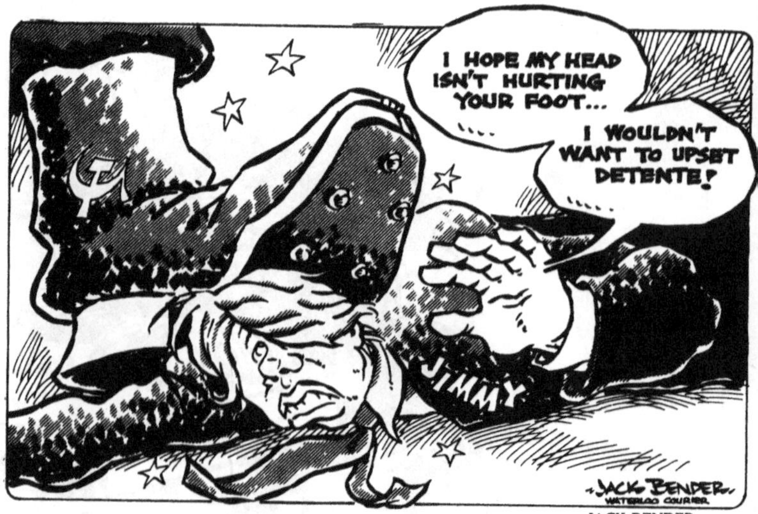
I HOPE MY HEAD ISN'T HURTING YOUR FOOT...
I WOULDN'T WANT TO UPSET DETENTE!
JIMMY
JACK BENDER
WATERLOO COURIER

JACK BENDER
Waterloo Courier
©Rothco Cartoons, Inc.

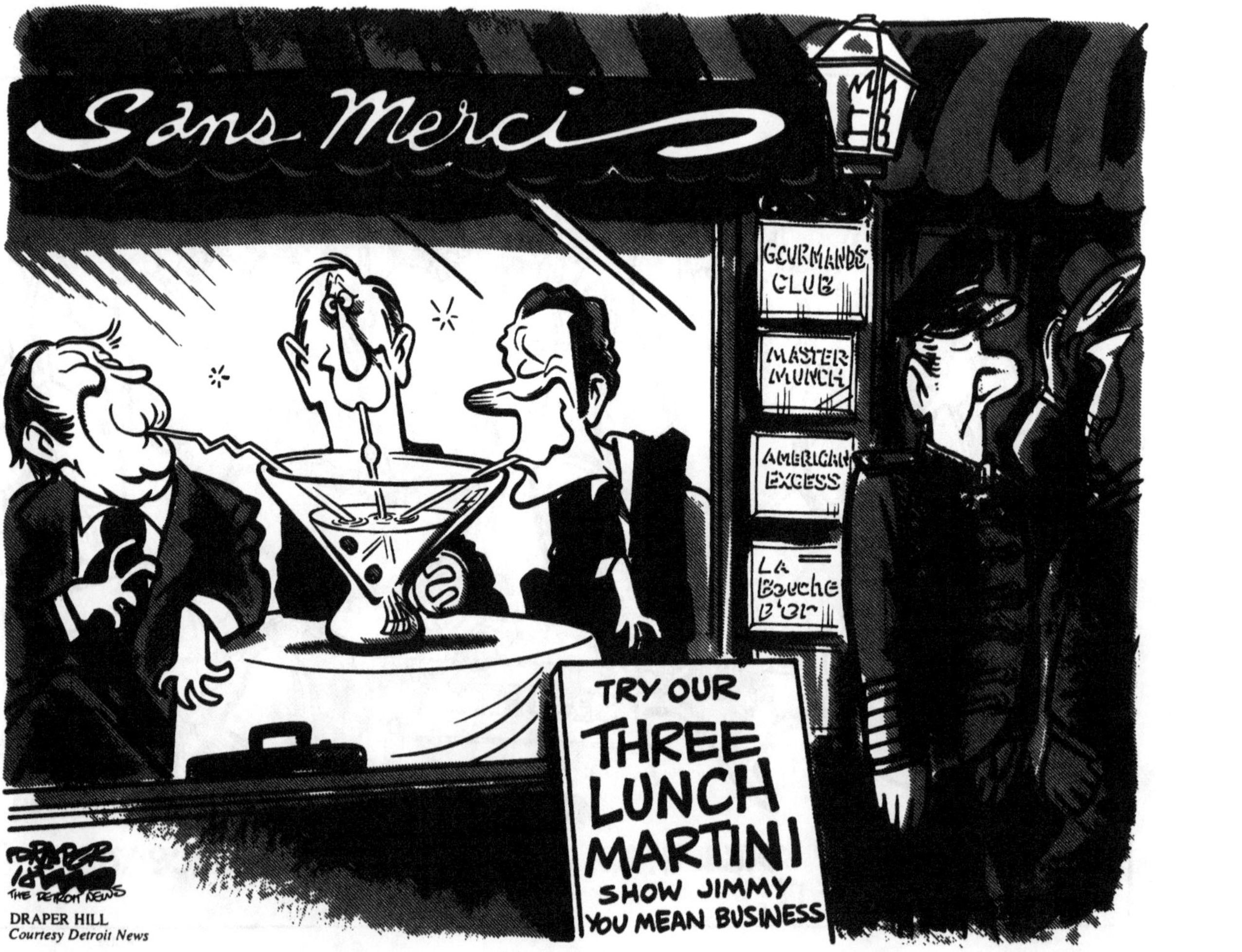
Sans Merci
GOURMANDS' CLUB
MASTER MUNCH
AMERICAN EXCESS
La Bouche
TRY OUR
THREE LUNCH MARTINI
SHOW JIMMY YOU MEAN BUSINESS
DRAPER HILL
THE DETROIT NEWS

DRAPER HILL
Courtesy Detroit News

PAUL SZEP
Courtesy Boston Globe

A POLITICIAN COMPANY SHOULD BE TRUSTWORTHY LOYAL HELPFUL FRIENDLY COURTEOUS KIND OBEDIENT CHEERFUL THRIFTY BRAVE CLEAN REVERENT

TOM CURTIS
Courtesy Milwaukee Sentinel

"Et tu, Bert . . . Andy . . . Hamilton . . . Andy . . . Dr. Bourne . . ."

FRANK INTERLANDI
©Los Angeles Times Syndicate

ROB LAWLOR
Courtesy Philadelphia Daily News

MIKE KONOPACKI
Madison Press Connection
©Rothco

SANDY CAMPBELL
Courtesy The Tennessean

THE WATER TRICK

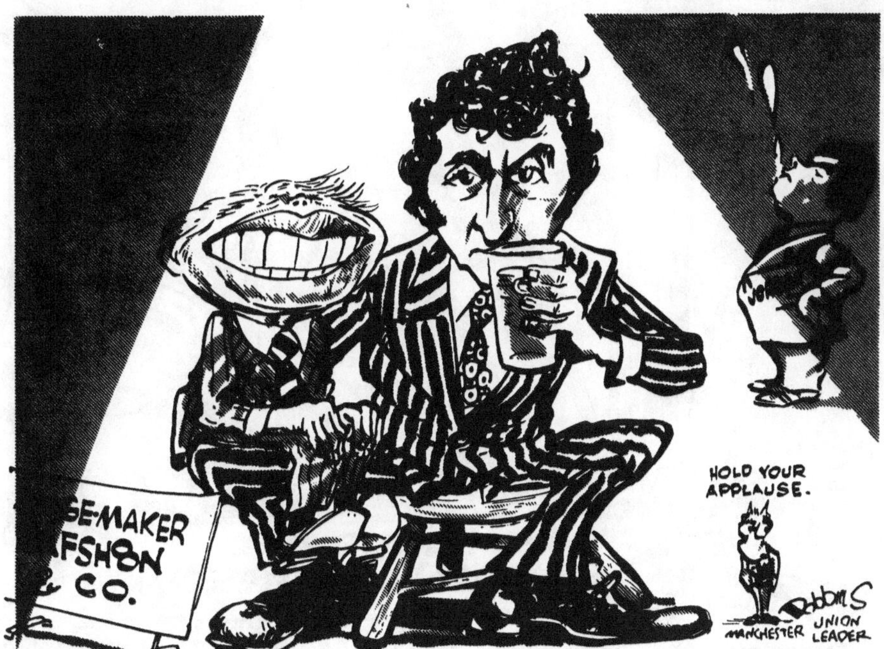
HOLD YOUR APPLAUSE.
MANCHESTER UNION LEADER

JIM DOBBINS
Courtesy Manchester Union-Leader

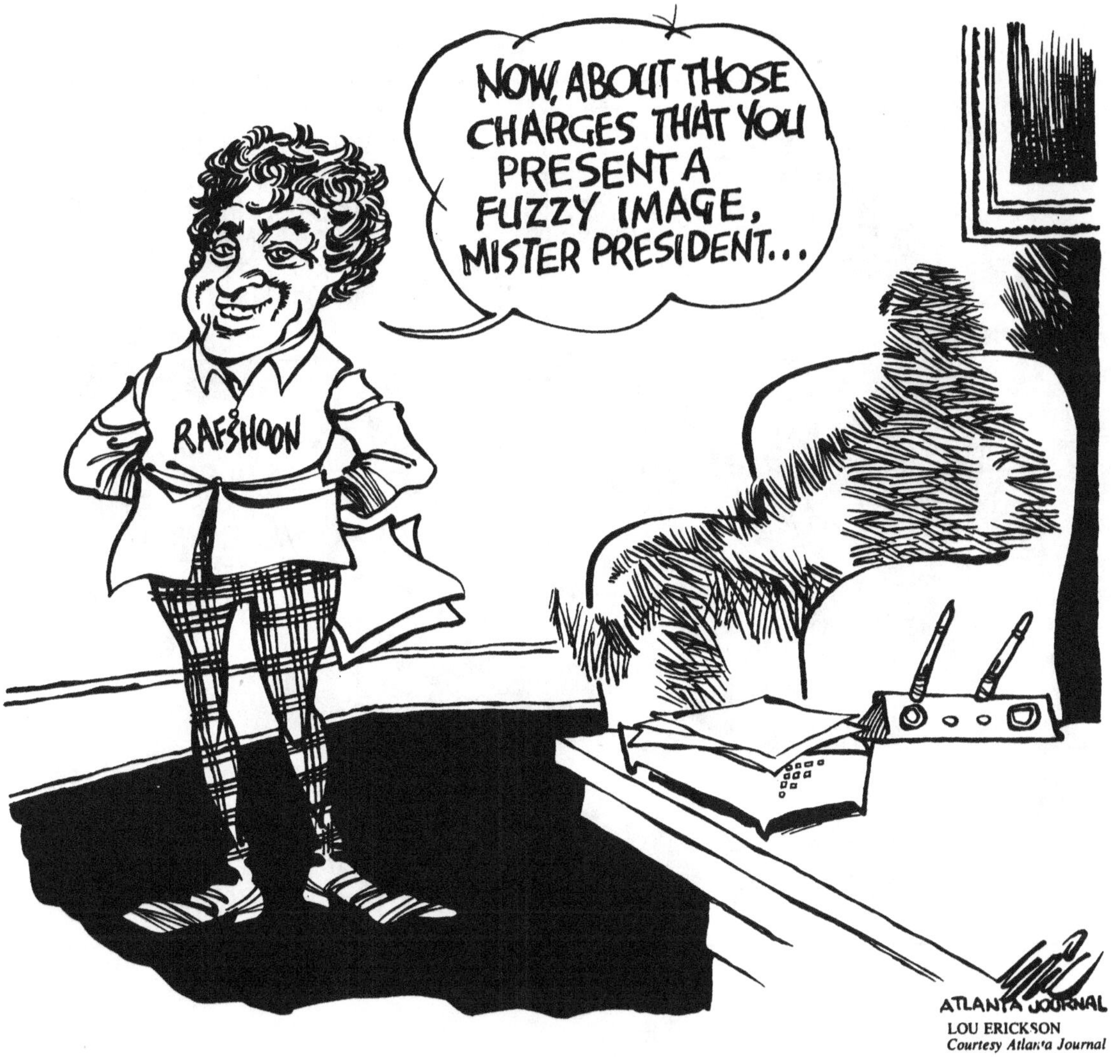
NOW, ABOUT THOSE CHARGES THAT YOU PRESENT A FUZZY IMAGE, MISTER PRESIDENT...
RAFSHOON
ATLANTA JOURNAL

LOU ERICKSON
Courtesy Atlanta Journal

DAVE GRANLUND
South Middlesex News
©Newspaper Enterprise Assn.

KATE PALMER
Courtesy Greenville (S.C.) News

JIM BORGMAN
Courtesy Cincinnati Enquirer

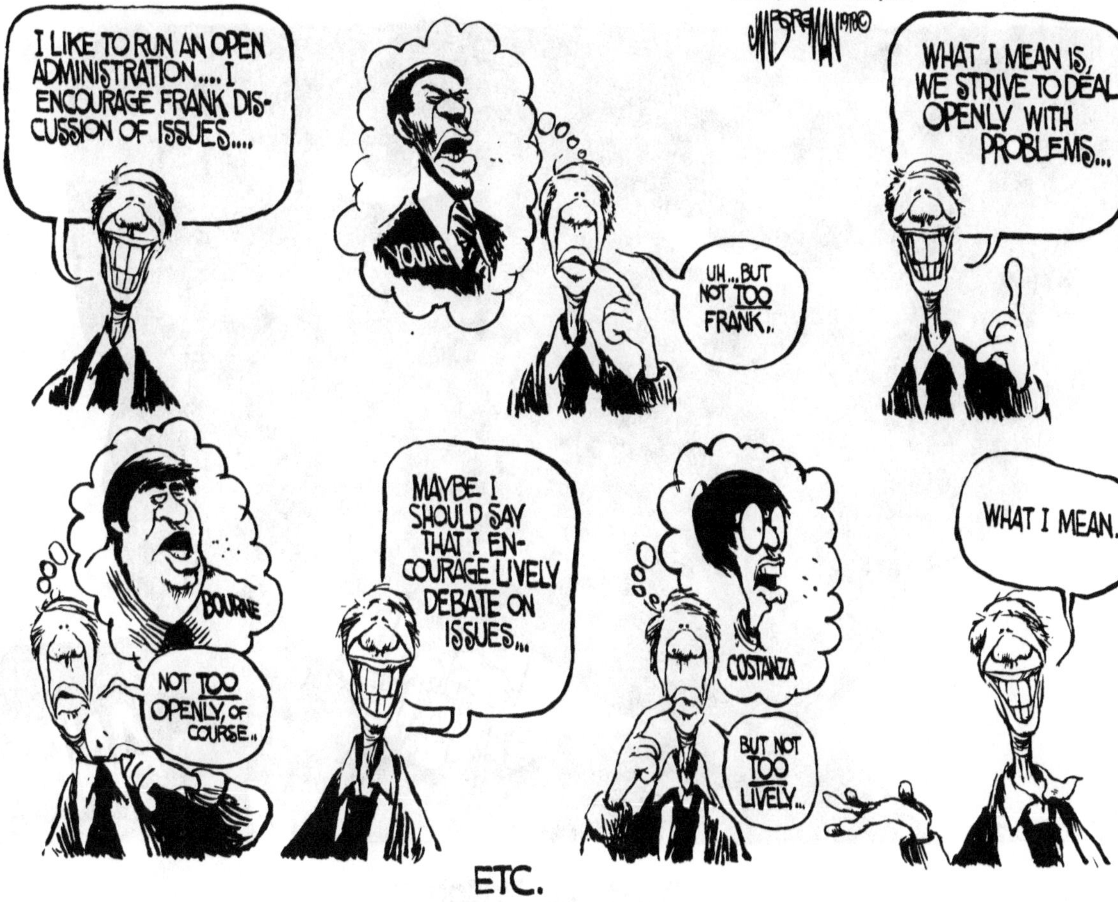

I LIKE TO RUN AN OPEN ADMINISTRATION.... I ENCOURAGE FRANK DISCUSSION OF ISSUES....
YOUNG
UH... BUT NOT TOO FRANK..
WHAT I MEAN IS, WE STRIVE TO DEAL OPENLY WITH PROBLEMS...
BOURNE
NOT TOO OPENLY, OF COURSE..
MAYBE I SHOULD SAY THAT I ENCOURAGE LIVELY DEBATE ON ISSUES...
COSTANZA
BUT NOT TOO LIVELY...
WHAT I MEAN..
ETC.

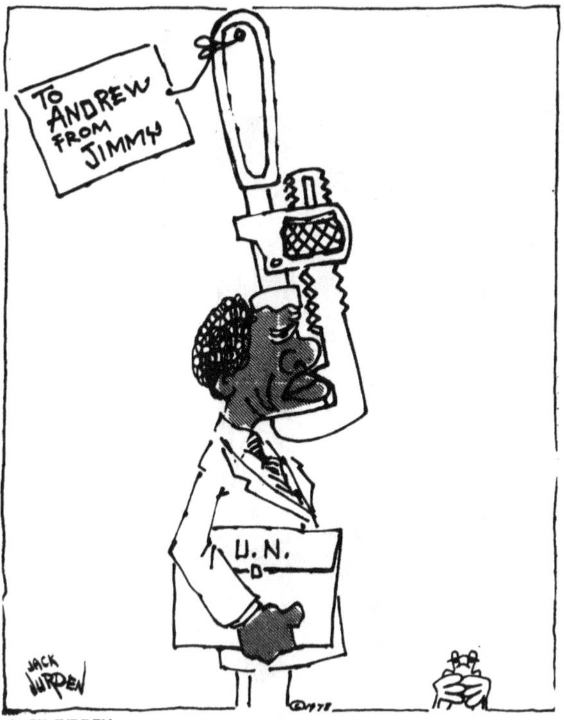

TO ANDREW FROM JIMMY
U.N.
JACK JURDEN

JACK JURDEN
Courtesy Wilmington Evening Journal-News

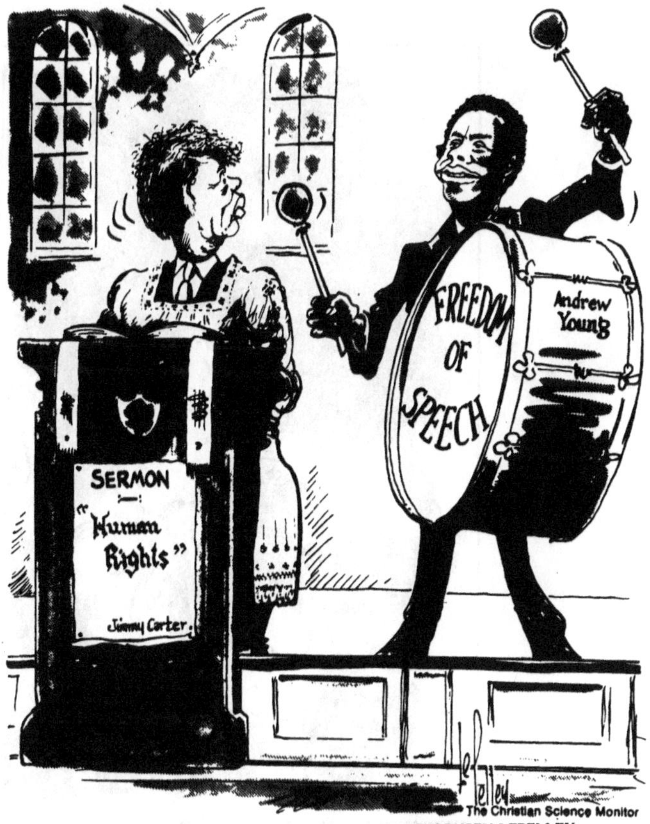

FREEDOM OF SPEECH
Andrew Young
SERMON
"Human Rights"
Jimmy Carter
The Christian Science Monitor

GUERNSEY LEPELLEY
Courtesy Christian Science Monitor

ANDY
WRIGHT THE PROVIDENCE JOURNAL-BULLETIN

DICK WRIGHT
Courtesy Providence Journal-Bulletin

Political Prisoner

CRASH
SQUAD
CARTER AND VANCE
QUIET ZONE
ANDY YOUNG
GULP
TIC-TOC
DIPLOMATIC TIMEBOMB
ATSEFF
© 1978 SYRACUSE HERALD-JOURNAL

TIMOTHY ATSEFF
Courtesy Syracuse Herald-Journal

Camp David—Mideast

In late November, 1977, President Anwar Sadat of Egypt startled the world by announcing that he would be willing to go anywhere—even to Israel—to further the prospects of peace between Arabs and Israelis. Prime Minister Begin accepted the offer and negotiations between the two were initiated. Sadat visited Jerusalem, thereby for the first time according official recognition to the State of Israel by an Arab country. After frank discussions, both sides went to work seeking a common ground for a lasting peace settlement.

Because of opposition in both countries, however, negotiations sputtered. In January, face-to-face talks were suspended. In an effort to breathe new life into the peace process, Vice President Walter Mondale visited both countries and urged a meeting of their foreign ministers. Such a meeting was later held in Great Britain, but it proved fruitless. Then, on August 8, President Carter announced that Begin and Sadat had accepted invitations to meet with Carter at the presidential retreat at Camp David, Maryland.

After two weeks of talks, the three leaders emerged to announce that a "framework for peace" had been reached. At year's end, however, the framework was still tenuous.

JIM MORIN
Courtesy Richmond Times-Dispatch

DWANE POWELL
Courtesy News and Observer

'SORRY, MR. ARAFAT, I DON'T SEE YOUR NAME LISTED — YOU SAY THAT'S WITH ONE T?'

CRAIG MACINTOSH
Courtesy Minneapolis Star

33

ANTHONY JENKINS
Courtesy Toronto Globe and Mail

NEW ISRAELI PEACE PROPOSAL INDICATES BEGIN MAY BE MOVING CLOSER TO CARTER-SADAT POSITIONS.

BOB TAYLOR
Courtesy Dallas Times Herald

BILL GARNER
Courtesy Memphis Commercial Appeal

JEFF MACNELLY
Richmond News Leader
©Chicago Tribune—New York
News Syndicate

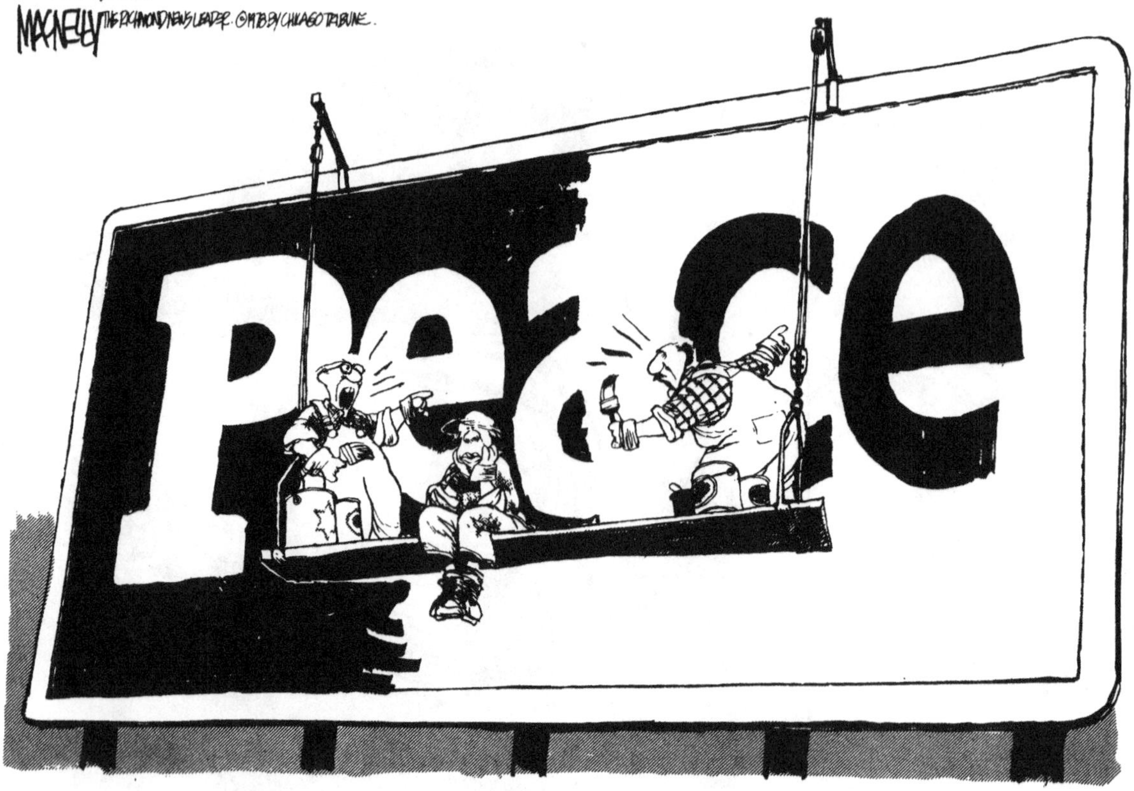
MACNELLY THE RICHMOND NEWS LEADER. ©1978 BY CHICAGO TRIBUNE.
Peace

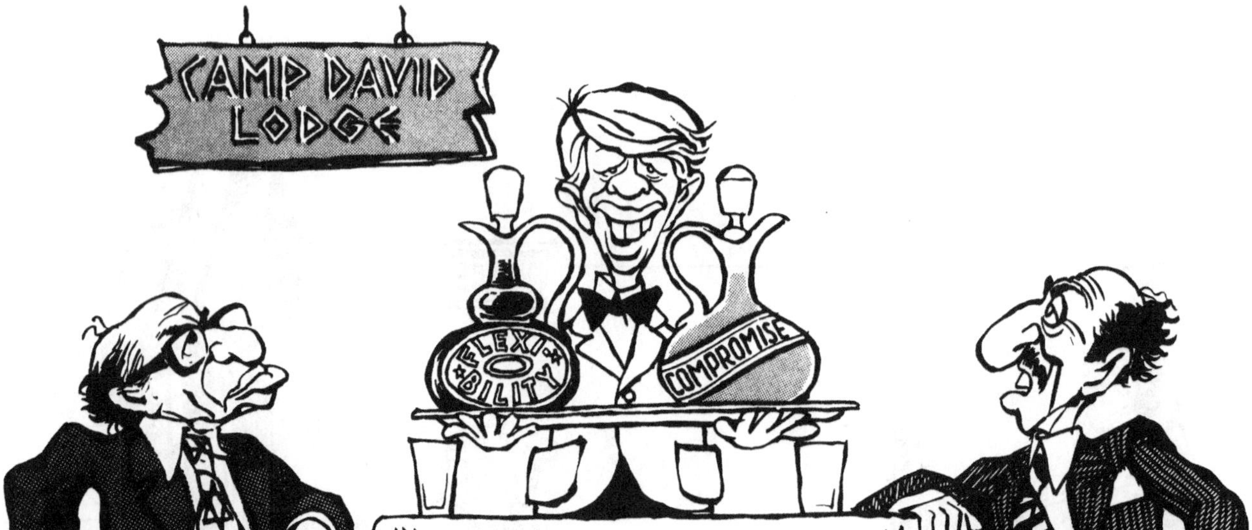
CAMP DAVID LODGE
FLEXI-BILITY
COMPROMISE
Valtman '78

'YOUR CHOICE, GENTLEMEN'

ED VALTMAN
©Rothco

"YOU'LL HAVE TO DROP SOMETHING TO SHAKE HANDS"

KARL HUBENTHAL
Courtesy Los Angeles Herald-Examiner

DENNIS RENAULT
Courtesy Sacramento Bee

"Jimmy Carter calls this a 'mobile' home; I just call it 'home'!"

FRANK INTERLANDI
©Los Angeles Times Syndicate

ROB LAWLOR
Courtesy Philadelphia Daily News

ANDY DONATO
Courtesy Toronto Sun

DOUGLAS BORGSTEDT
©Copley News Service

'NOW THEN, WHO'S GONNA BLINK FIRST?'

CAMP DAVID   EVEN A FAINT SQUINT WILL DO

CHARLES WERNER
Courtesy Indianapolis Star

"Trouble with YOU is, you're stubborn!"

EUGENE CRAIG
Courtesy Columbus (O.) Dispatch

DAVID WILEY MILLER
Courtesy Press Democrat,
Santa Rosa, Cal.

JIMMY MARGULIES
©Rothco Cartoons

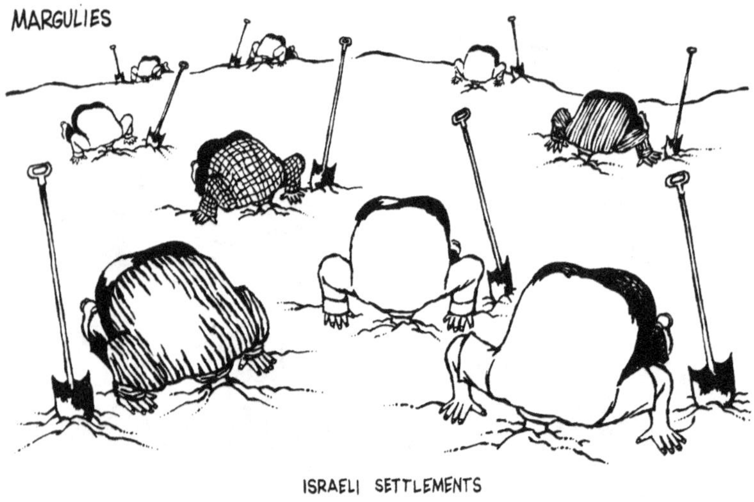
MARGULIES
ISRAELI SETTLEMENTS

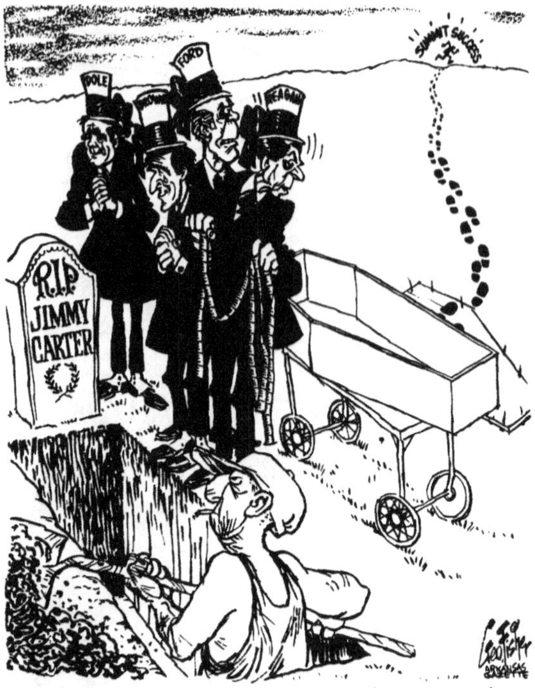
SUMMIT SUCCESS
DOLE
FORD
REAGAN
R.I.P.
JIMMY
CARTER

GEORGE FISHER
Courtesy Arkansas Gazette

S. C. RAWLS
Courtesy Palm Beach Post

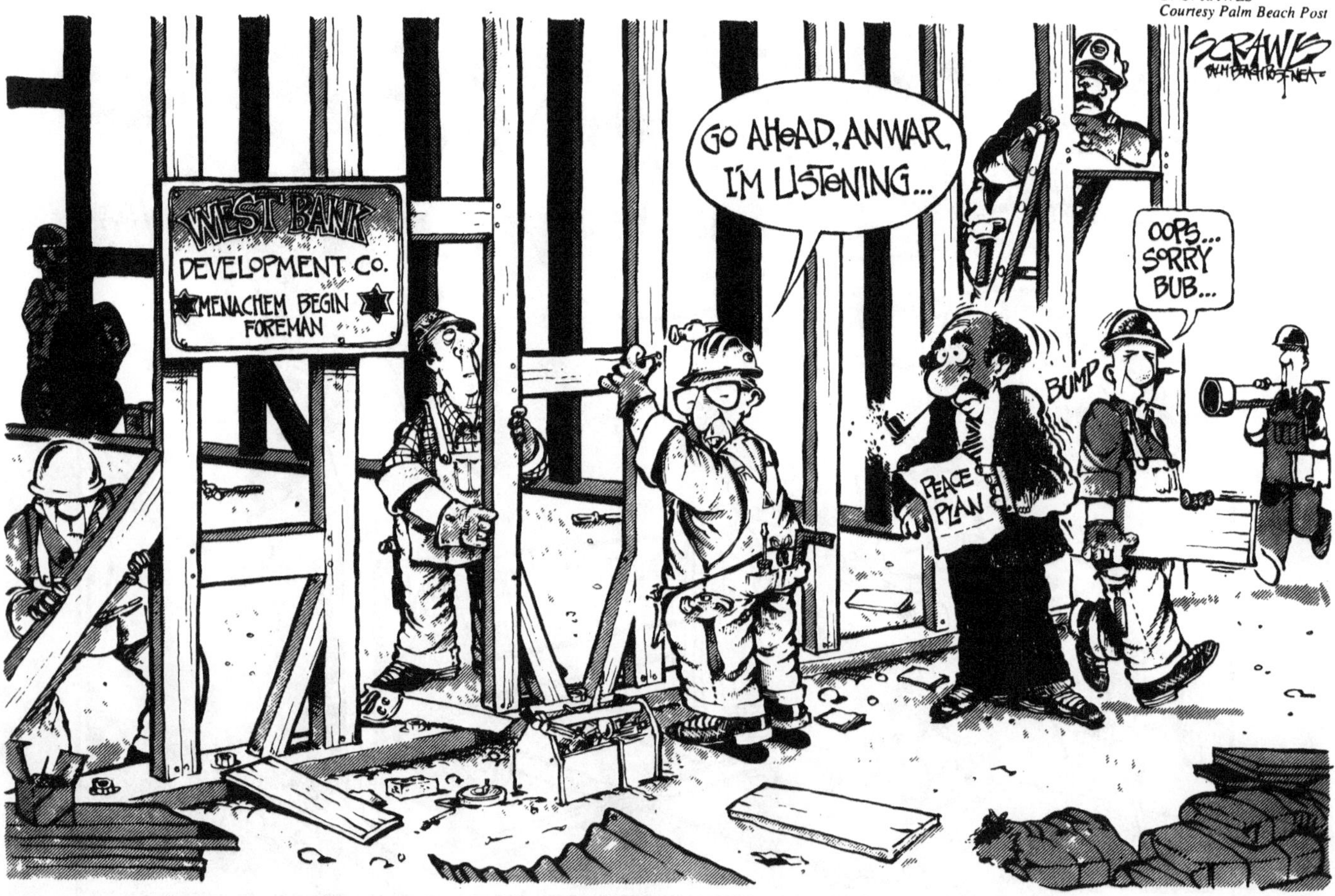
SCRAWLS
GO AHEAD, ANWAR, I'M LISTENING...
WEST BANK
DEVELOPMENT CO.
MENACHEM BEGIN
FOREMAN
OOPS... SORRY BUB...
BUMP
PEACE PLAN

JACK McLEOD
Courtesy Buffalo Evening News

JACK LANIGAN
Courtesy New Bedford Standard-Times

THE MAGIC OF CAMP DAVID

DANA SUMMERS
Courtesy Fayetteville
(N. C.) Times

'Just stay ready — we could dispatch you at any time'

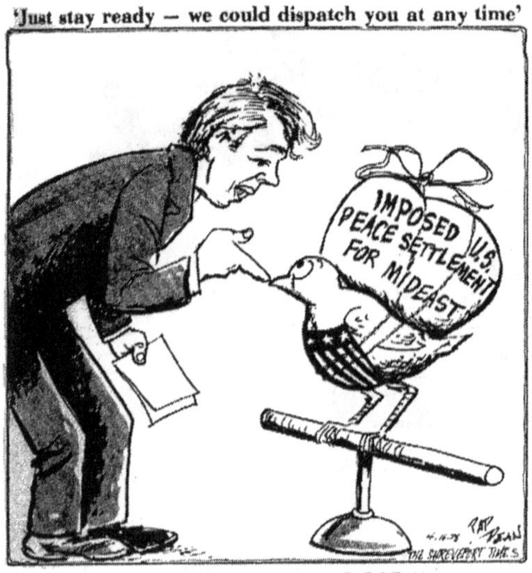
IMPOSED U.S. PEACE SETTLEMENT FOR MIDEAST
THE SHREVEPORT TIMES

PAP DEAN
Courtesy Shreveport Times

JOHN CRAWFORD
Courtesy Alabama Journal

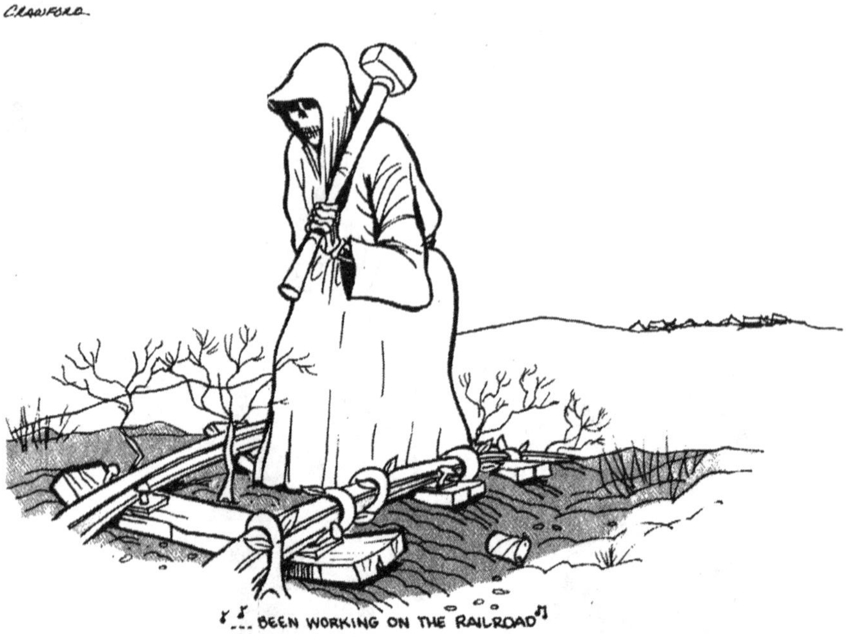
CRAWFORD
... BEEN WORKING ON THE RAILROAD

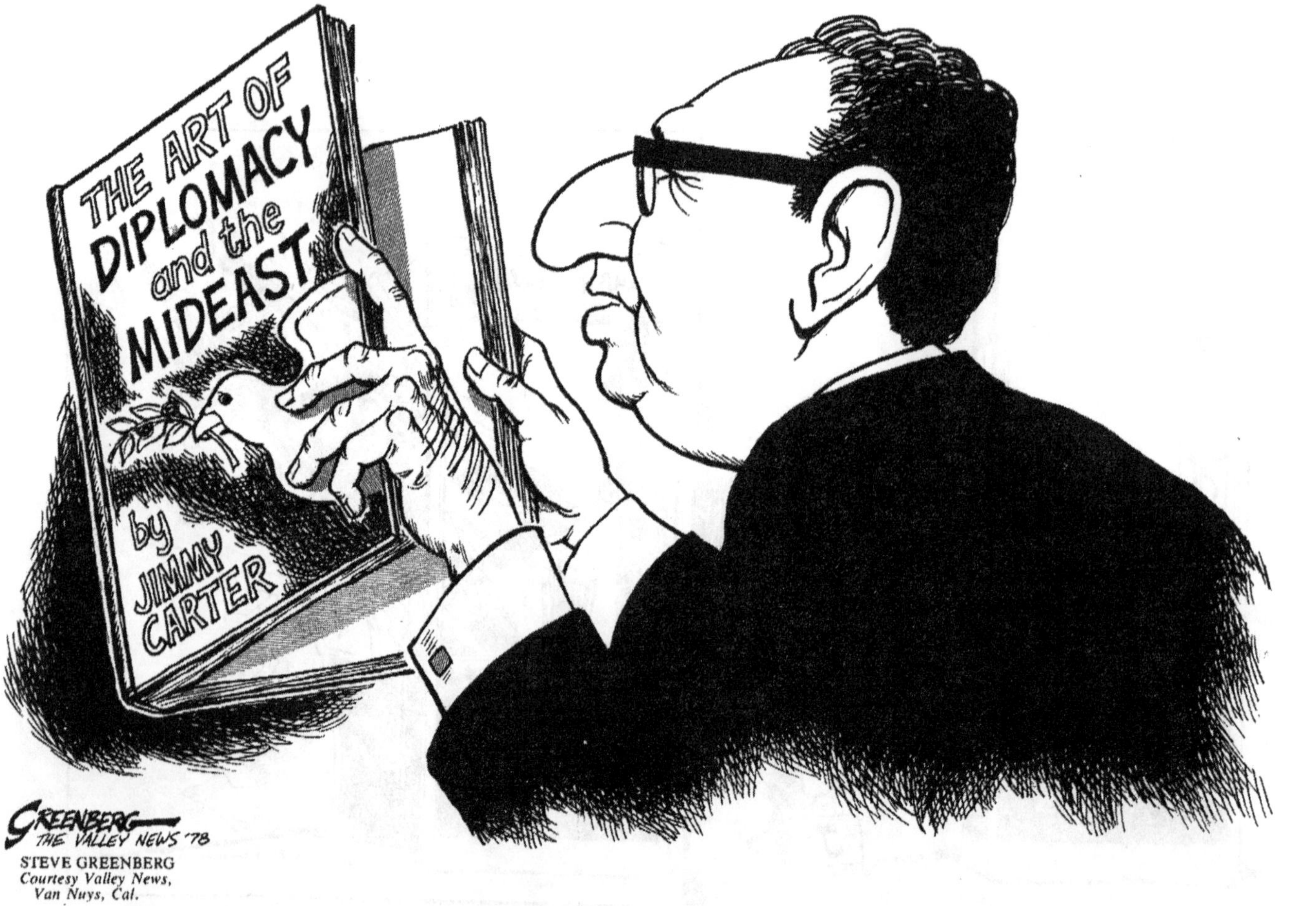
THE ART OF DIPLOMACY and the MIDEAST
by JIMMY CARTER
GREENBERG
THE VALLEY NEWS '78

STEVE GREENBERG
Courtesy Valley News, Van Nuys, Cal.

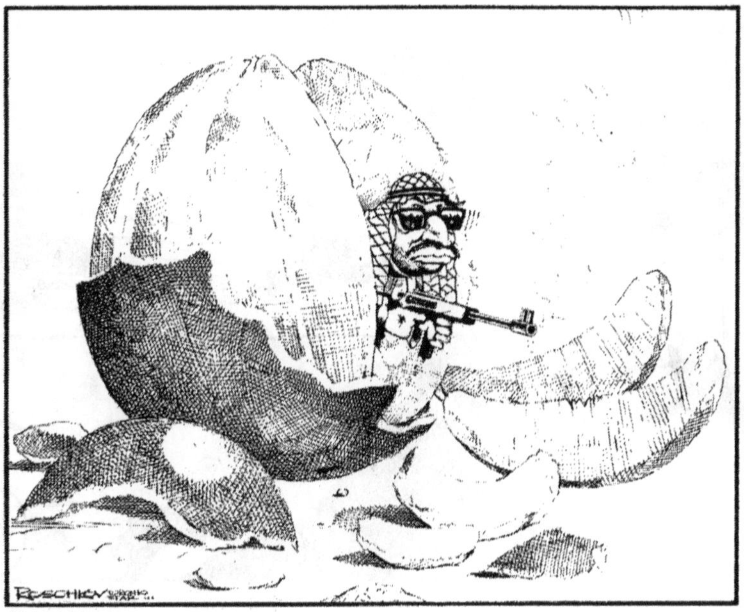
ROSCHKOV

VIC ROSCHKOV
Courtesy Toronto Star

POISON

BOB TAYLOR
Courtesy Dallas Times Herald

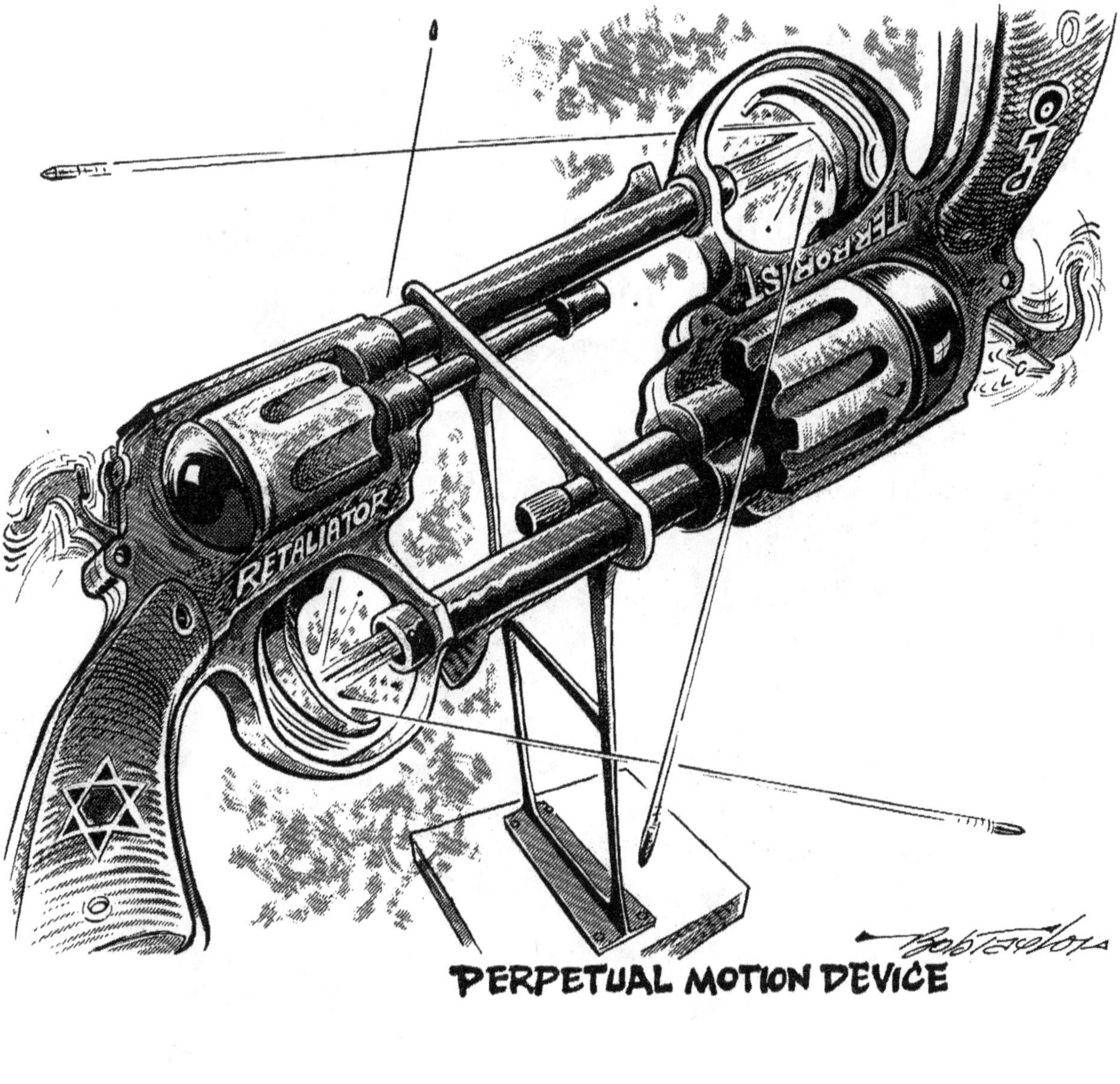
TERRORIST
RETALIATOR
PLO

PERPETUAL MOTION DEVICE

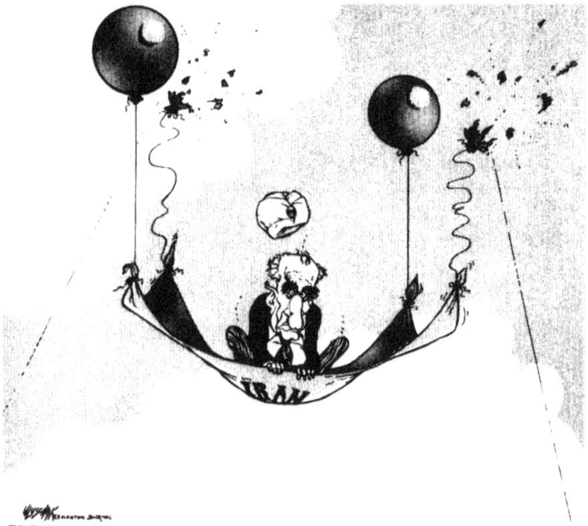
IRAN

EDD ULUSCHAK
Courtesy Edmonton Journal

GENE BASSET
Courtesy Scripps-Howard Newspapers

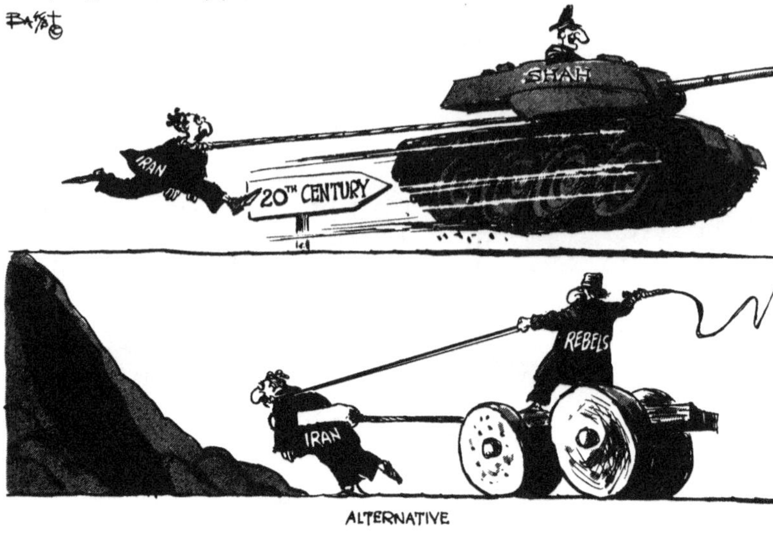
SHAH
IRAN
20TH CENTURY
REBELS
IRAN
ALTERNATIVE

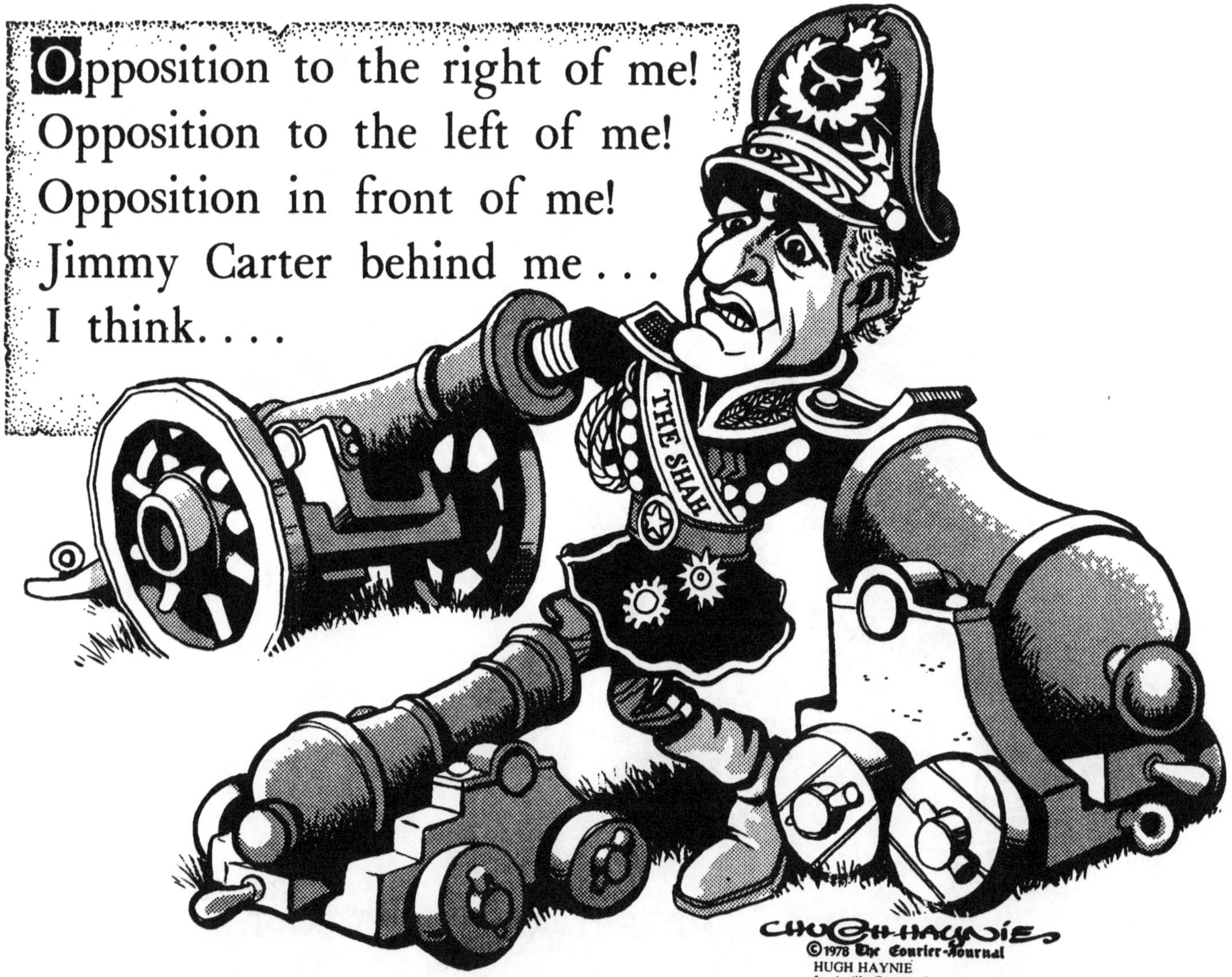
Opposition to the right of me!
Opposition to the left of me!
Opposition in front of me!
Jimmy Carter behind me . . .
I think. . . .
THE SHAH
HUGH HAYNIE
©1978 The Courier-Journal

HUGH HAYNIE
Louisville Courier-Journal
©Los Angeles Times Syndicate

JERRY ROBINSON
©Cartoonists and Writers
Snydicate

DOUG SNEYD
©Sneyd Syndicate

Politics

Political positions of officeholders and would-be officeholders changed dramatically across the nation after the controversial Proposition 13 in California passed easily in June. Voters there approved a statewide property tax cut of about $7 billion annually.

Almost immediately after the vote, most office-seekers began to sound like rigid fiscal conservatives. It seemed as if each was trying to outdo the other with promises of tax reductions and belt-tightening in government.

As expected, the party in power lost seats in the November elections. The losses, however, were not as severe as usual, and Democratic strength remained overwhelming in both houses of Congress—58 to 41 in the Senate (with one Independent) and 277 to 158 in the House of Representatives.

It became clear, however, that voters had become fed up with waste in government and were beginning to demand better services for their tax money.

Ronald Reagan barnstormed through 26 states speaking in behalf of Republican candidates and appeared to be the early frontrunner for the GOP nomination for president in 1980. On the Democratic side, most polls showed Senator Ted Kennedy of Massachusetts as the favorite for the Democratic nomination over Jimmy Carter in 1980.

KARL HUBENTHAL
Courtesy Los Angeles Herald-Examiner

PAUL SZEP
Courtesy Boston Globe

JERRY BARNETT
Courtesy Indianapolis News

JIM DOBBINS
Courtesy Manchester Union-Leader

JIM BORGMAN
Courtesy Cincinnati Enquirer

HAVE FENCE, WILL TRAVEL

LOU GRANT
Oakland Tribune
©Los Angeles Times Syndicate

JERRY ROBINSON
©Cartoonists and Writers Snydicate

RAY OSRIN
Courtesy Cleveland Plain Dealer

PAUL SZEP
Courtesy Boston Globe

TIP O'NEILL

Great Slogans in History

JIM PALMER
Courtesy Dallas News

America's Economy

Financial markets and institutions in the U.S. experienced a generally prosperous year in 1978. It was nevertheless a turbulent year economically, however, with inflation rising to around the 10 percent mark, the dollar continuing a headlong slide, and interest rates soaring.

The banking industry registered impressive gains in earnings. The Federal Reserve, under new chairman, G. William Miller, took a series of steps designed to raise interest rates and therefore dampen money-supply growth, on which inflation feeds.

The nation's civilian unemployment rate declined to about 6 percent in 1978, down from 7 percent the previous year. More than three million persons entered the work force during the year, bringing the total employed to around 100 million. The percentage of the population over age 16 in the labor force reached an all-time high of 63.3 percent during the year.

Economic growth was tempered by the longest coal strike in history, lasting from December 6, 1977 to March 24, 1978. Farmers took to the highways to protest the economic squeeze in which they found themselves, many of them driving their tractors to Washington, D.C. to dramatize their plight.

BILL GARNER
Courtesy Memphis Commercial Appeal

JACK JURDEN
Courtesy Wilmington Evening Journal-News

ELDON PLETCHER
New Orleans Times-Picayune
©Rothco

TOM CURTIS
Courtesy Milwaukee Sentinel

"Hail to the Chief"

October Massacre

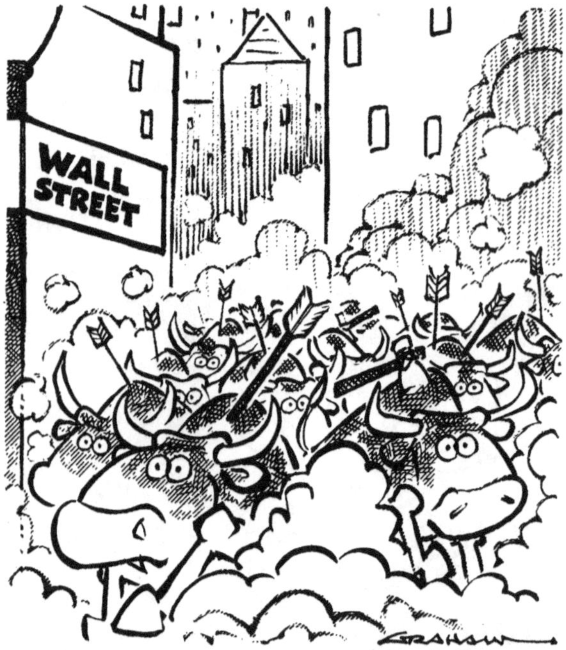
WALL STREET
GRAHAM

BILL GRAHAM
Courtesy Arkansas Gazette

WATCH OUT FOR OVERKILL!

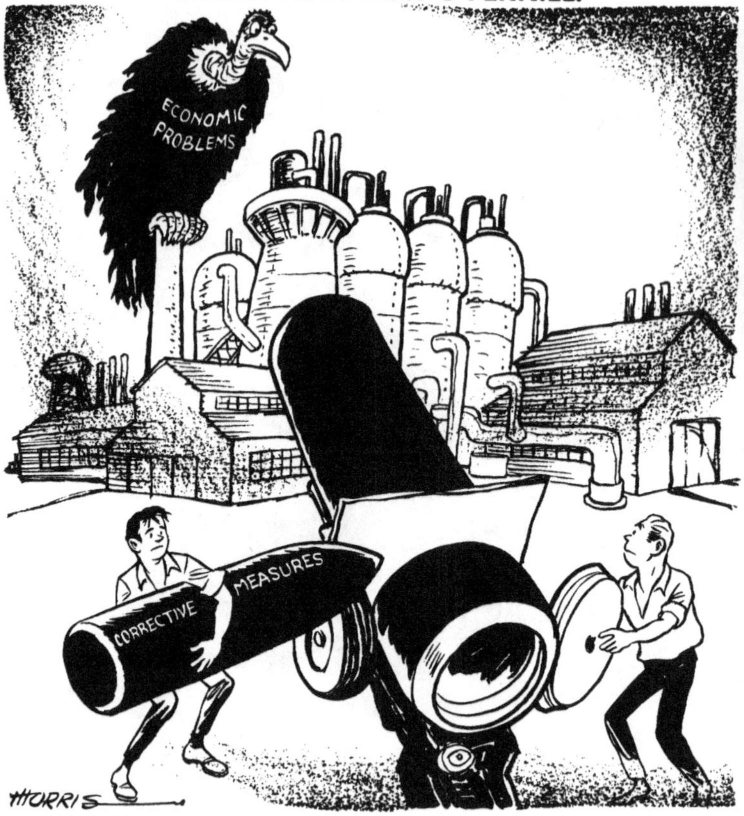
ECONOMIC PROBLEMS
CORRECTIVE MEASURES
MORRIS

JOHN MILT MORRIS
©The Associated Press

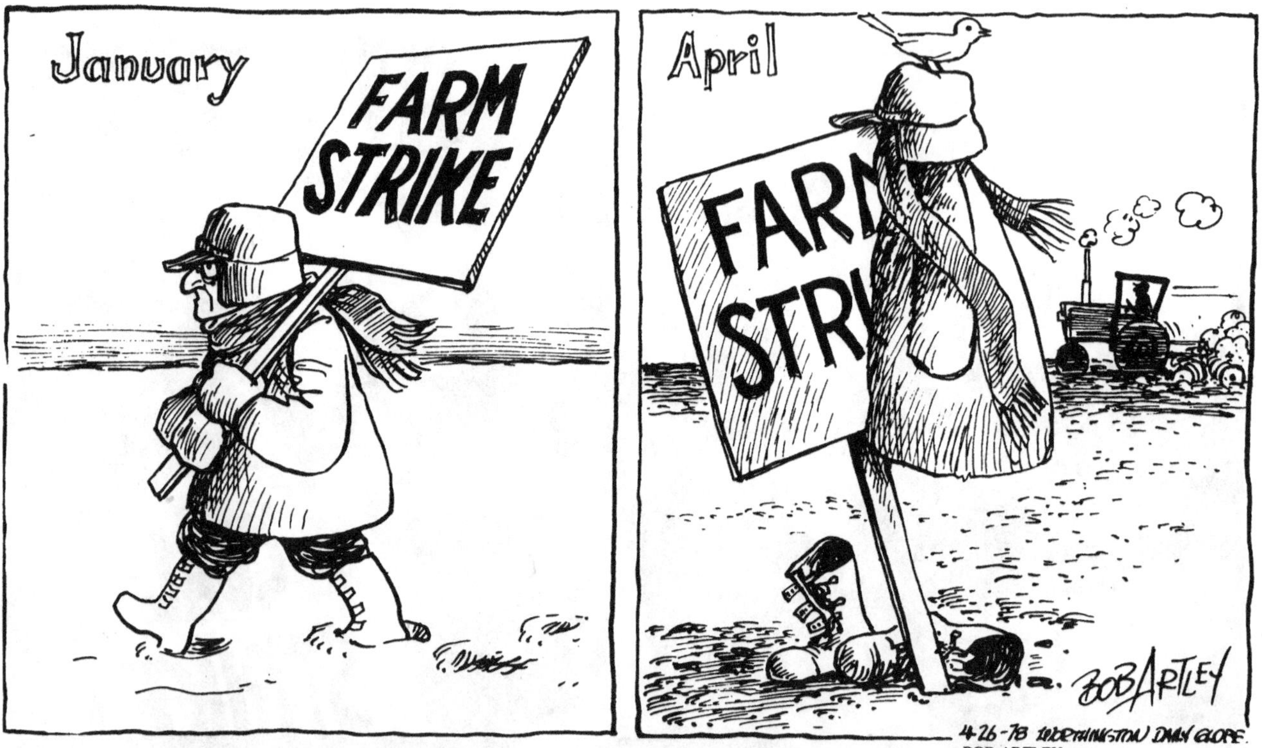
January
FARM STRIKE
April
FARM STRI
BOB ARTLEY
4-26-78 WORTHINGTON DAILY GLOBE

BOB ARTLEY
Courtesy Worthington (Minn.) Daily Globe

FRANCIS BRENNAN
©Newsweek

ART WOOD
Courtesy Farm Bureau News

SANDY CAMPBELL
Courtesy The Tennessean

DWANE POWELL
Courtesy News and Observer

WE TOLD YOU IT'D NEVER FLY!
INFLATION PLAN
AFL-CIO
POWELL

WAGE DEMANDS
PRICES
I'll lower mine when he lowers his ....
INDUSTRY
AFL-CIO
©1978 CHICAGO TRIBUNE
LOCHER

DICK LOCHER
Courtesy Chicago Tribune

THANK YOU, MR. PRESIDENT!

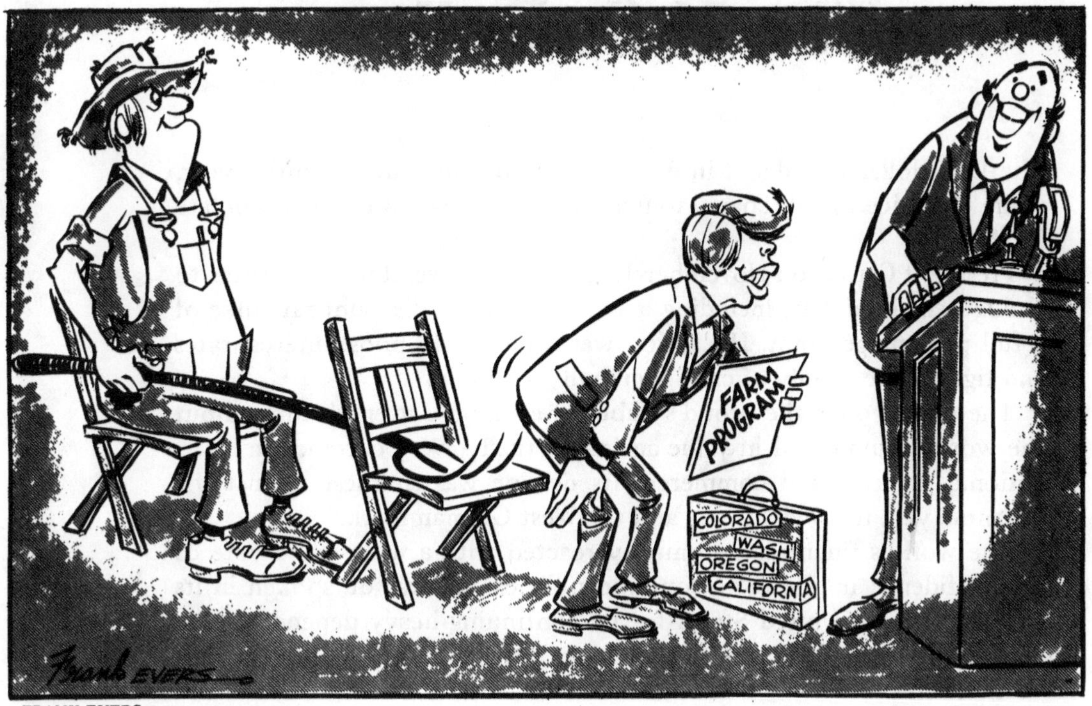
FARM PROGRAM
COLORADO
WASH
OREGON
CALIFORNIA
Frank EVERS

FRANK EVERS
Courtesy N. Y. Daily News

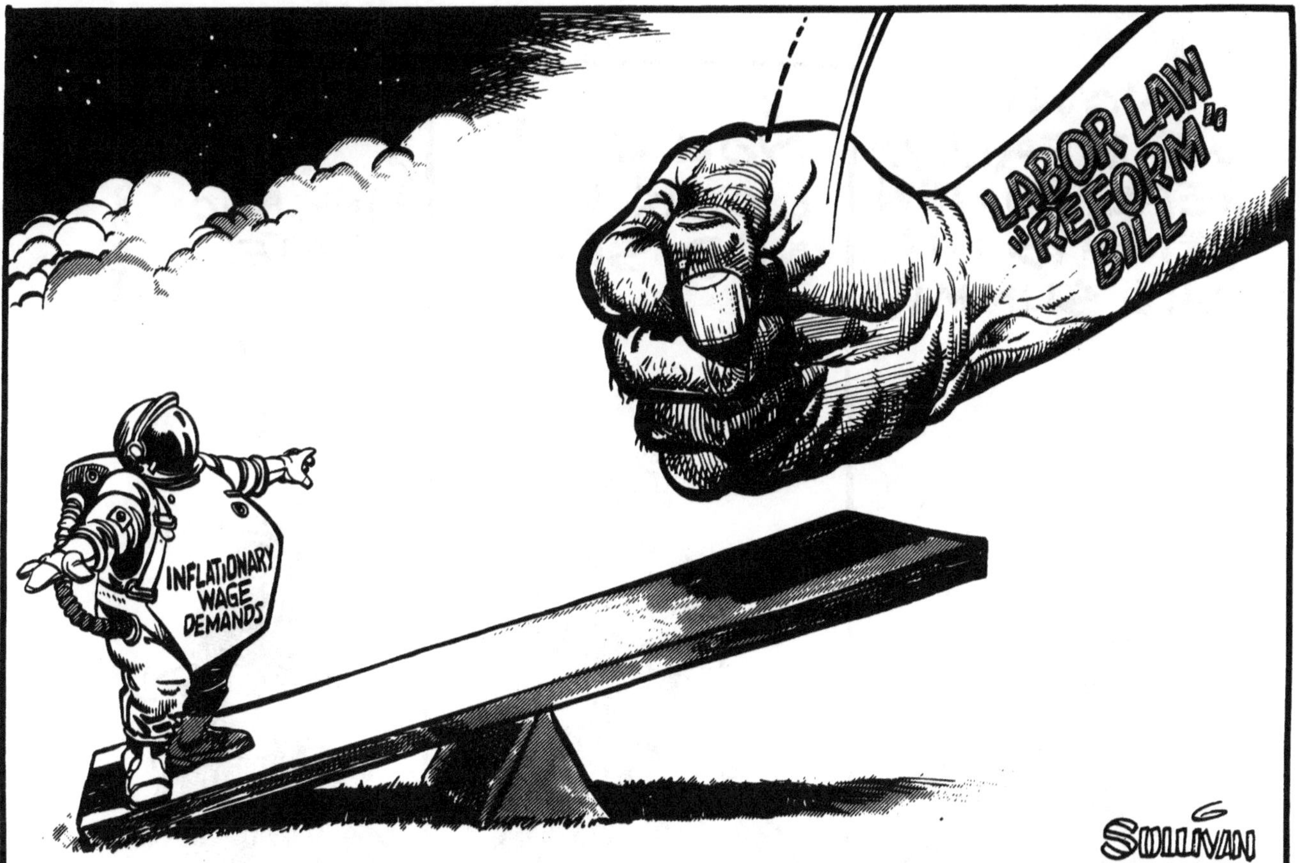
LABOR LAW "REFORM" BILL
INFLATIONARY WAGE DEMANDS
SULLIVAN

F.I.S.T.

BOB SULLIVAN
Courtesy Worcester Telegram

The U.S. Dollar

The U.S. dollar foundered in deep trouble throughout the entire year, while the price of gold soared well above the $200-an-ounce mark in late 1978.

President Carter, on November 1, announced several new measures to strengthen the dollar, including a Federal Reserve discount rate hike of a full percentage point. His action was intended to boost interest rates and tighten the supply of credit generally available.

The dollar, once the proud symbol of economic strength throughout the world, plummeted in value against virtually every currency in international banking and commerce. Its decline was sharpest against the Japanese yen, the Swiss franc, and the West German mark.

The world's financial community reacted with a widespread vote of no confidence in Carter's economic policies and was outspoken in its criticism of the United States for its continuing heavy dependence on foreign oil.

Inflation pressures were felt much more acutely during 1978 than in the previous year. Food costs increased at an annual rate of about 14 percent, while housing rose 12 percent. Studies showed that about 40 percent of the average American's income was spent for shelter.

CHARLES DANIEL
Courtesy Knoxville Journal

KEVIN McVEY
Courtesy The Record, Hackensack, N.J.

ART WOOD
Courtesy Farm Bureau News

JOHN SHEVCHIK
Courtesy Beaver Falls (Pa.) News Tribune

JOHN STAMPONE
Courtesy Army Times

ELDON PLETCHER
New Orleans Times-Picayune
©Rothco

NEW ROLE

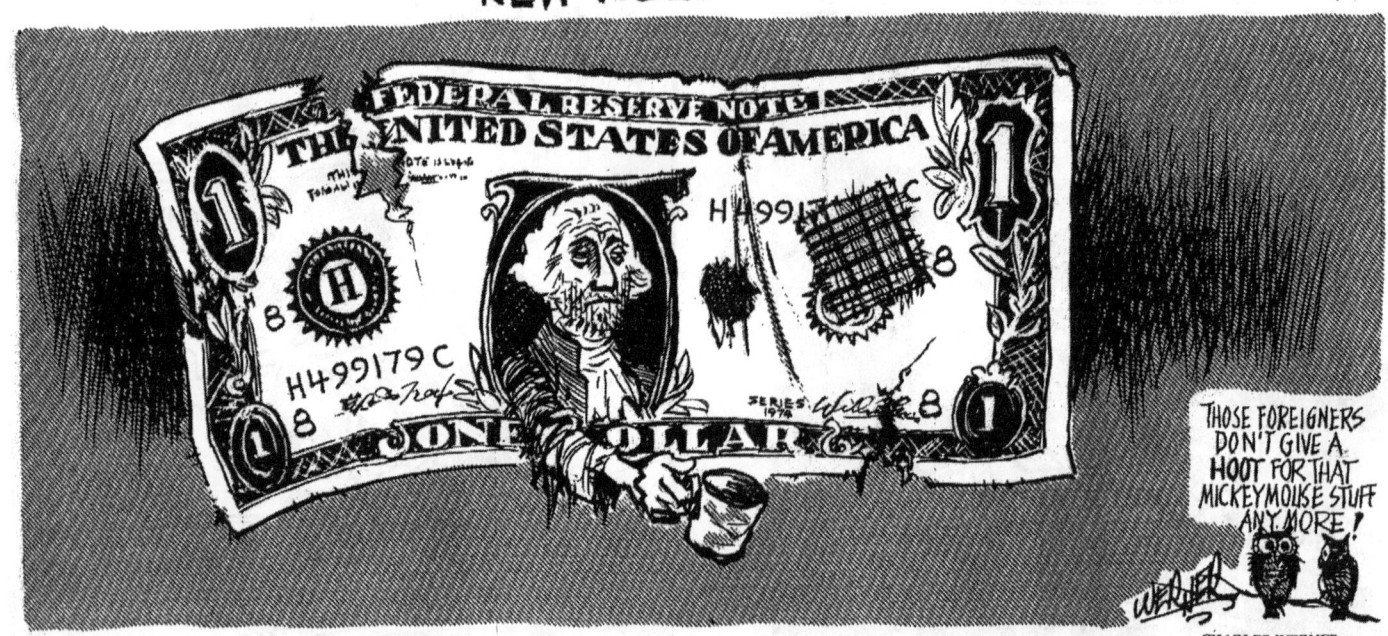

CHARLES WERNER
Courtesy Indianapolis Star

STEPHEN SACK
Courtesy Ft. Wayne Journal

KARL HUBENTHAL
Courtesy Los Angeles Herald-Examiner

"BANZAI!"

ED ASHLEY
Courtesy Toledo Blade

THE DOLLAR SINKS TO A NEW LOW

JIM LANGE
The Daily Oklahoman
©The Oklahoma Publishing Co.

"Help a Vet?"

TOM FLANNERY
Courtesy Baltimore Sun

"PEASANT!"

HY ROSEN
Courtesy Albany Times-Union

ART HENRIKSON
©Paddock Publications

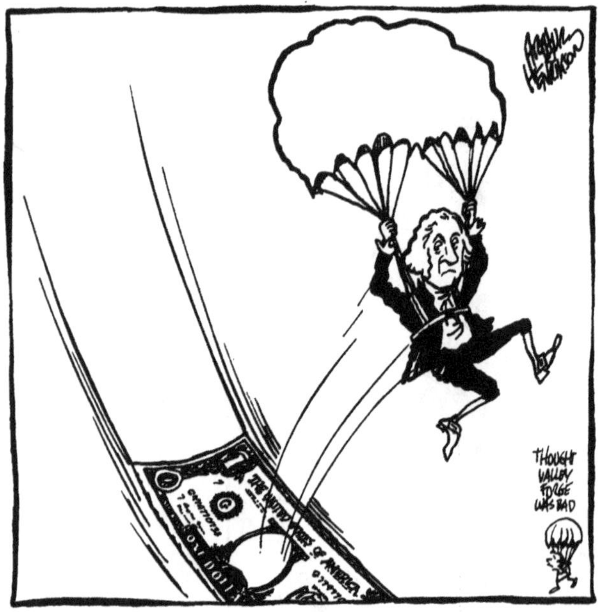
THOUGHT VALLEY FORGE WAS BAD

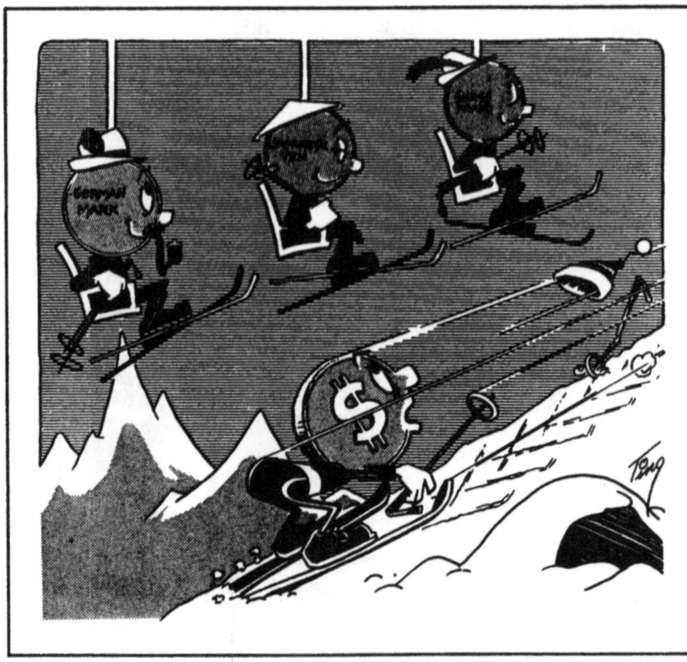

MERLE TINGLEY
Courtesy London (Can.) Free Press

MIKE KEEFE
Courtesy Denver Post

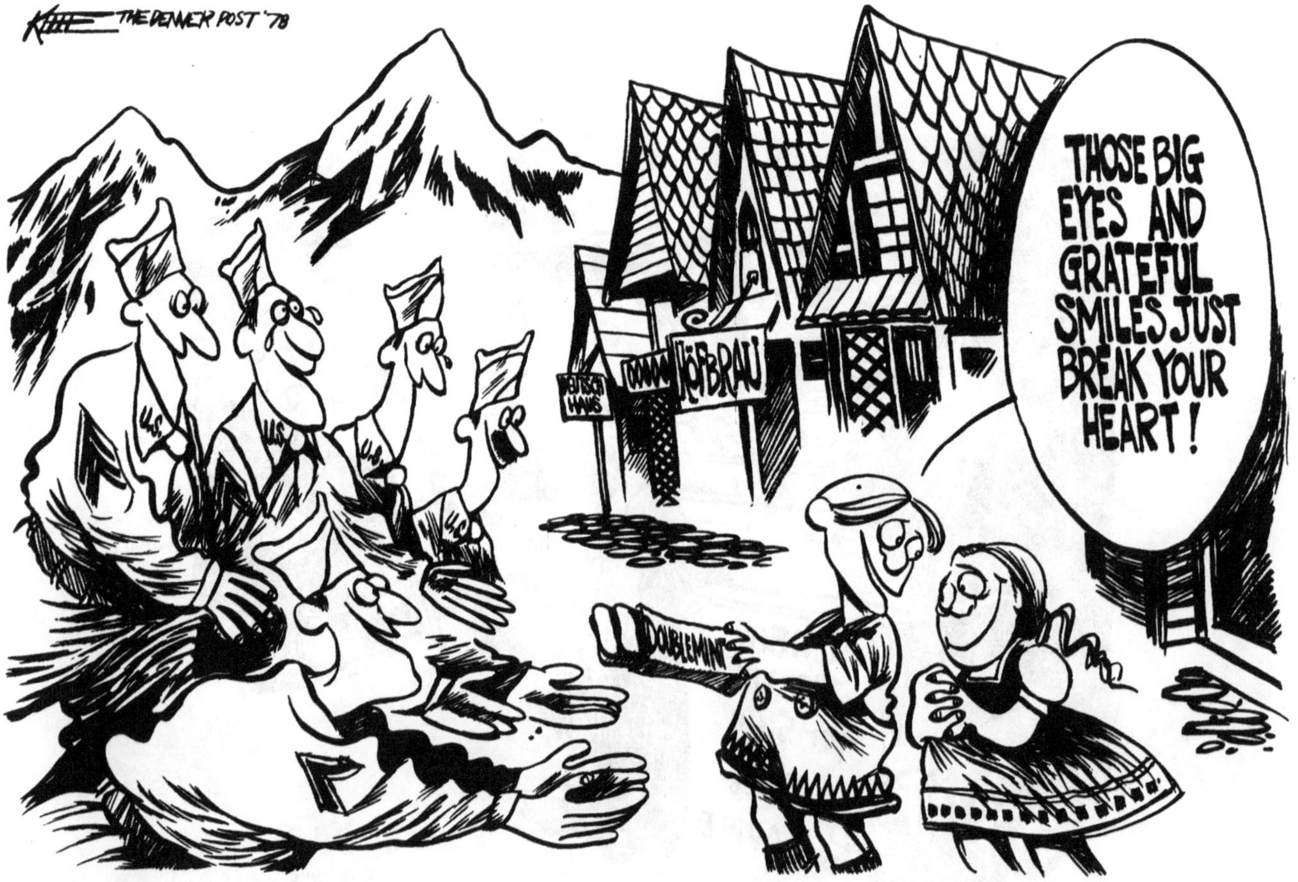
THE DENVER POST '78
DEUTSCH HAUS
HOFBRAU
DOUBLEMINT
THOSE BIG EYES AND GRATEFUL SMILES JUST BREAK YOUR HEART!

EUGENE CRAIG
Courtesy Columbus (O.) Dispatch

VERN THOMPSON
Courtesy Lawton (Okla.) Constitution

JOHN PIEROTTI
Courtesy Atlantic City Press

DANA SUMMERS
Courtesy Fayetteville (N. C.) Times

FRANK EVERS
Courtesy N. Y. Daily News

EDD ULUSCHAK
Courtesy Edmonton Journal

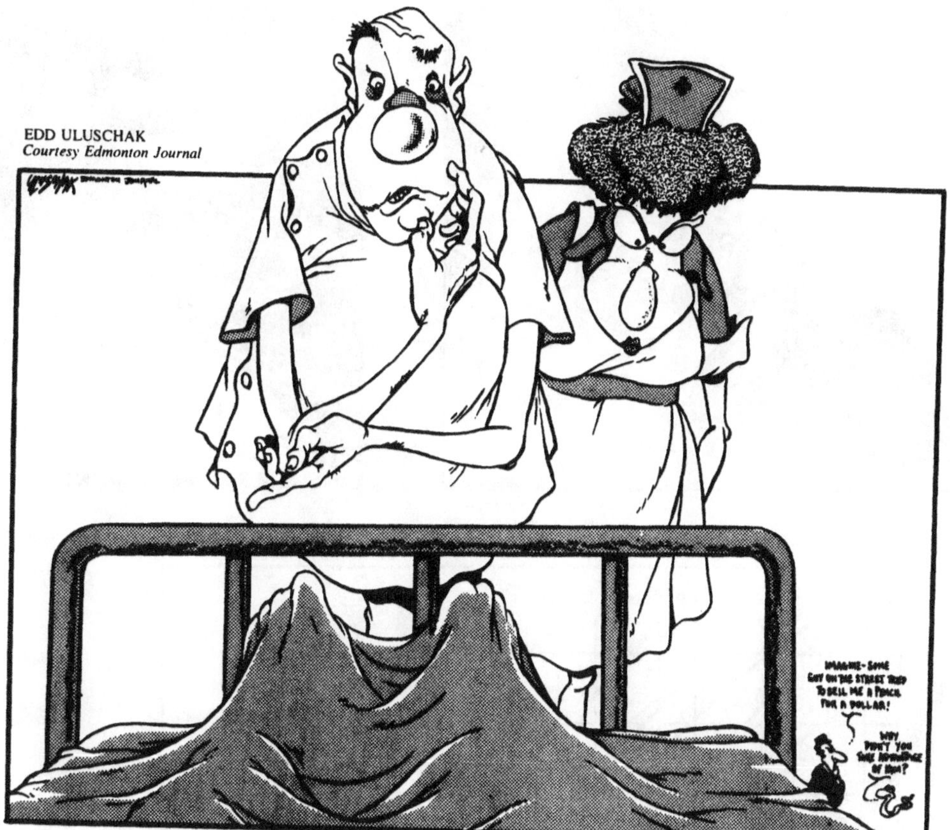
IMAGINE—SOME GUY ON THE STREET TRIED TO SELL ME A PEACH FOR A DOLLAR!
WHY DIDN'T YOU TAKE ADVANTAGE OF HIM?

"He died of fright right after I told him he was as sound as a dollar!"

CLYDE WELLS
Courtesy Augusta (Ga.) Chronicle

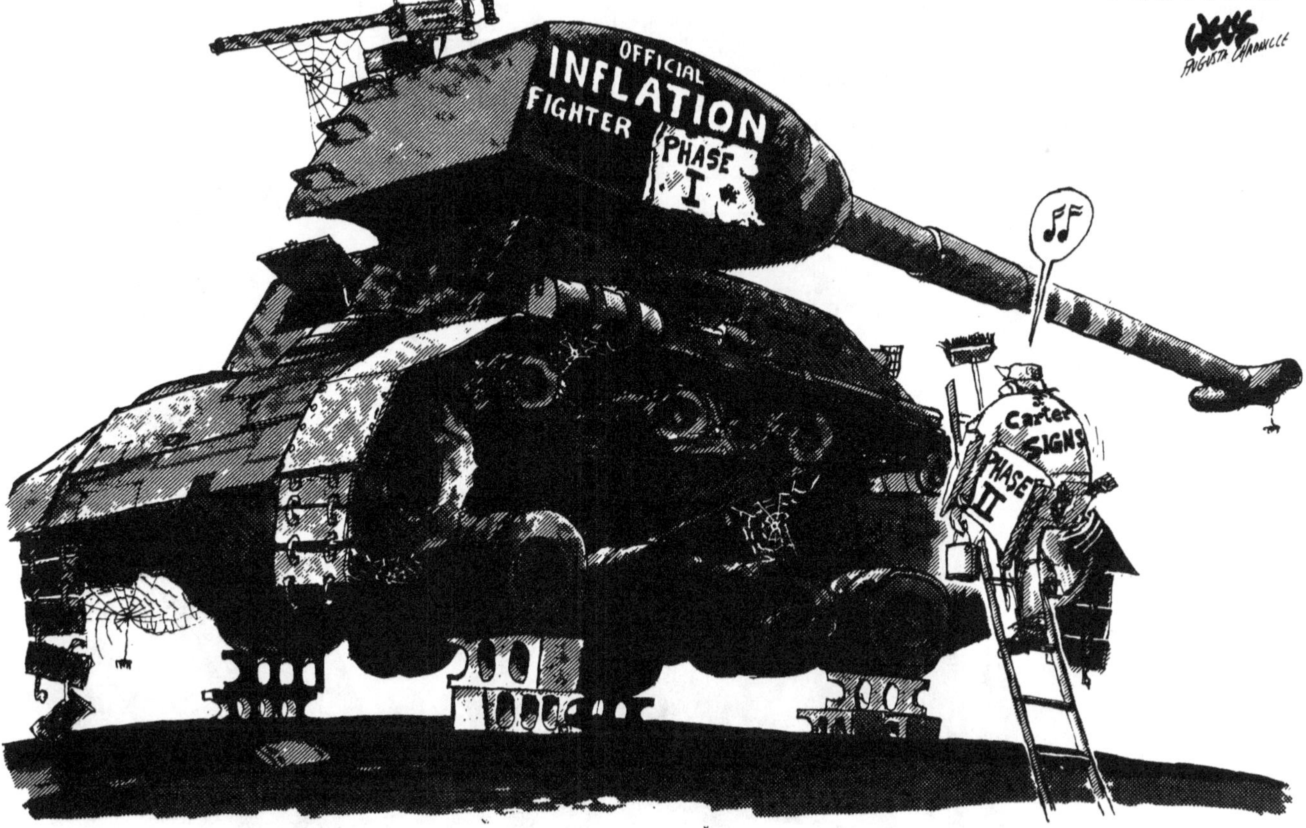
OFFICIAL INFLATION FIGHTER
PHASE I
Carter SIGNS
PHASE II

NO RELIEF IN SIGHT

SANDY CAMPBELL
Courtesy The Tennessean

RAY OSRIN
Courtesy Cleveland Plain Dealer

"...AND SO, AS THE DOLLAR SINKS SLOWLY IN THE WEST, WE SAY FAREWELL..."

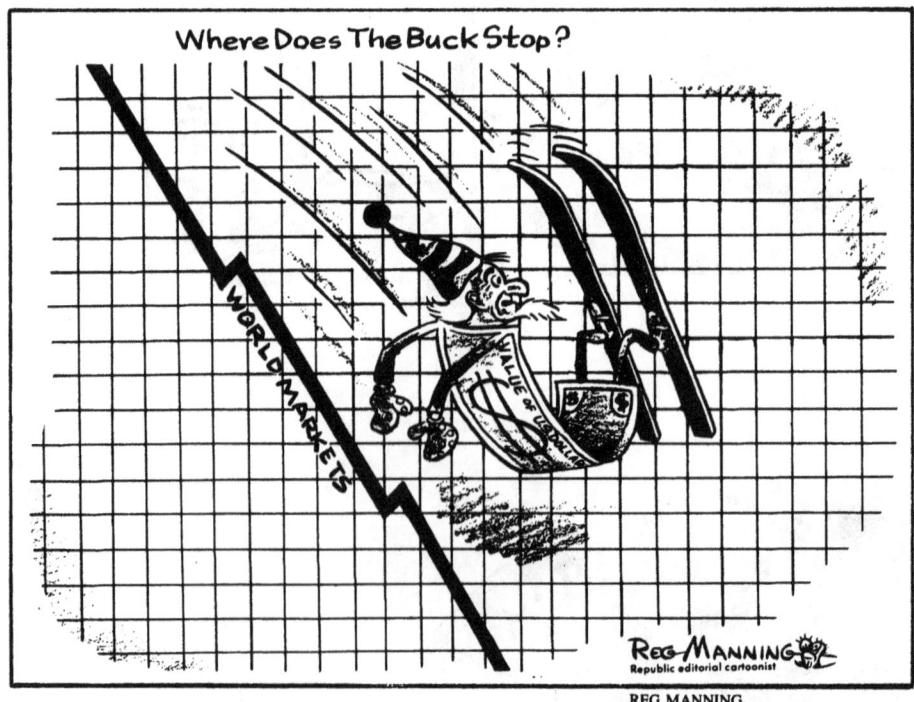

REG MANNING
Courtesy Arizona Republic

ED GAMBLE
Courtesy Nashville Banner

SNAKE EYES !!!

VERN THOMPSON
Courtesy Lawton (Okla.) Constitution

DOUGLAS BORGSTEDT
©Copley News Service

"Smelling salts and wheelchair ready? I'm about to hit the total."

Foreign Affairs

Much of the year found the Carter Administration reacting to Russian and Cuban moves in troubled Africa. The Castro regime gave high priority to a growing military role in support of leftist groups virtually halfway around the world. Most of the Cuban presence was felt in Angola and Ethiopia.

In a challenging speech on July 26, Castro announced that his relationship with the so-called Third World was much more important to his government than his relationship with the United States. His remarks surprised some observers since President Carter had been making overtures toward normalizing relations with Cuba.

Much of the world was stunned by Carter's announcement in December that, effective the first of the year, the U.S. would recognize Red China as the only "real" China. After the initial shock subsided, many applauded the move as realistic, while others saw it as a disgraceful act of treaty-breaking and abandonment of a proven ally, Taiwan.

Riots and disorders aimed at deposing the Shah of Iran grew steadily and by year's end had almost paralyzed the nation. Opposing the long-reigning Shah were Moslem conservatives who felt his program of modernization had moved too fast and leftist students who clamored for more freedoms.

CLYDE WELLS
Courtesy Augusta (Ga.) Chronicle

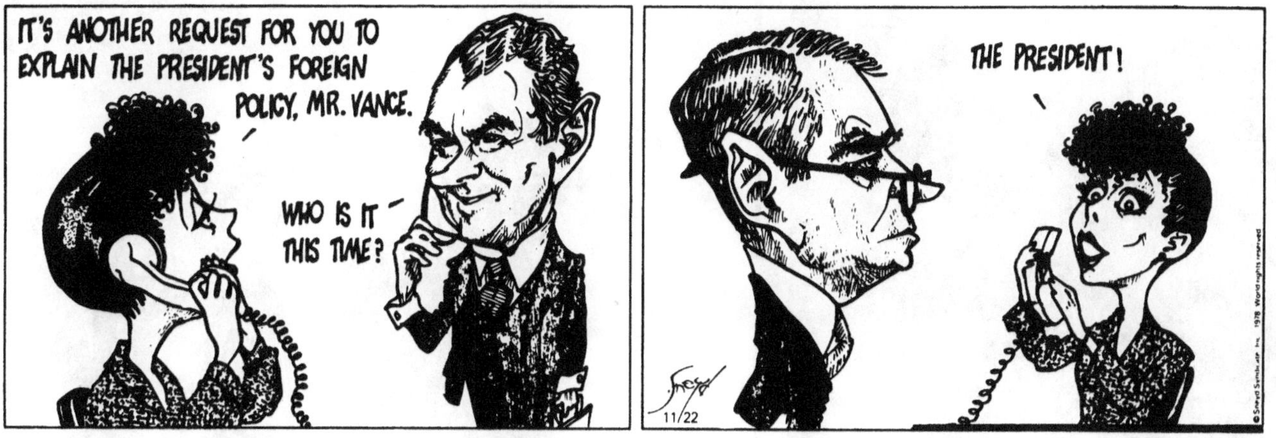
IT'S ANOTHER REQUEST FOR YOU TO EXPLAIN THE PRESIDENT'S FOREIGN POLICY, MR. VANCE.
WHO IS IT THIS TIME?
THE PRESIDENT!
11/22

DOUG SNEYD
©Sneyd Syndicate

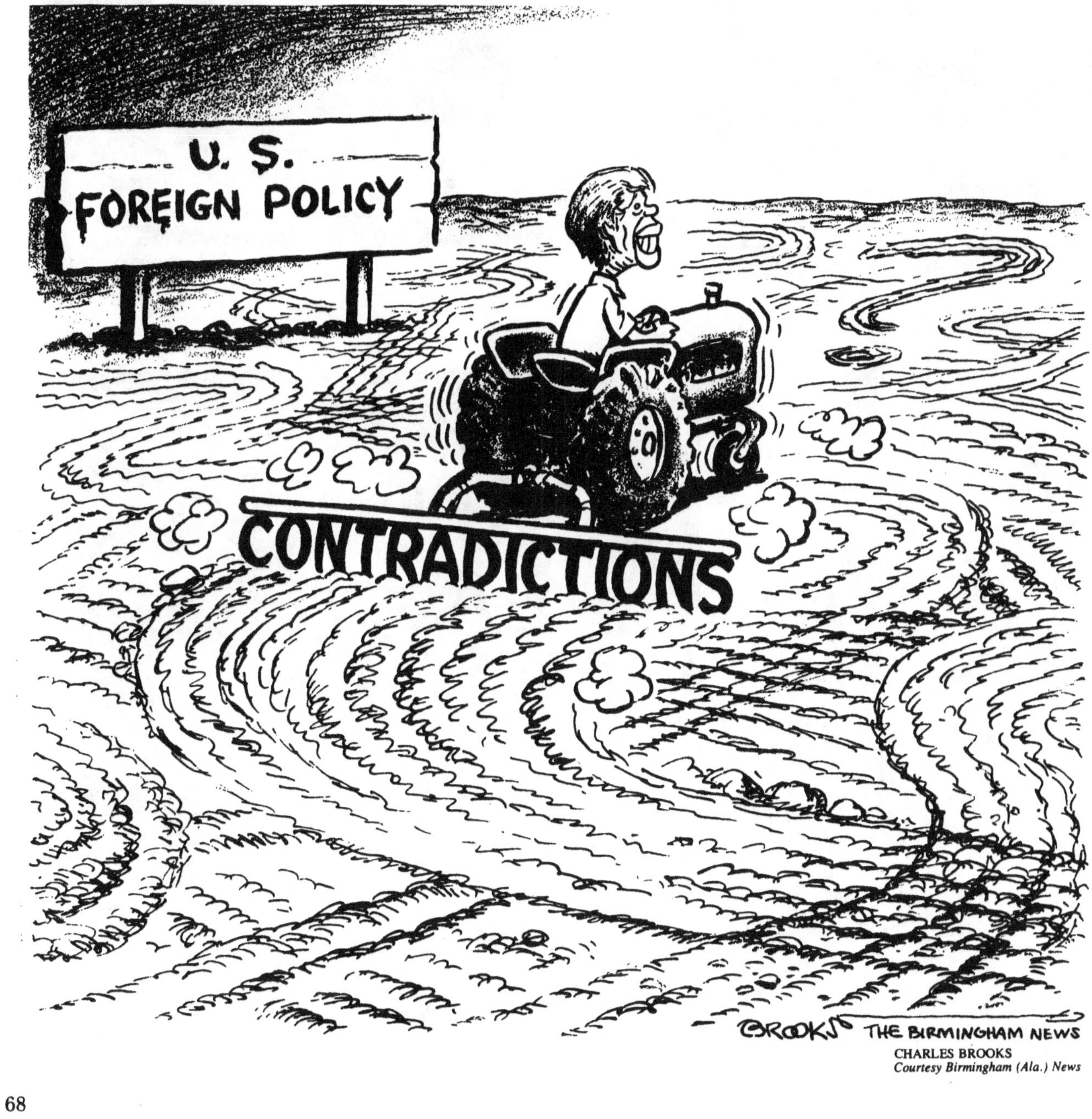
U. S. FOREIGN POLICY
CONTRADICTIONS
THE BIRMINGHAM NEWS

CHARLES BROOKS
Courtesy Birmingham (Ala.) News

Pietà

DANI AGUILA
Courtesy Filipino Reporter

'Mamma, she's Italian'

GUERNSEY LEPELLEY
Courtesy Christian Science Monitor

CHUCK AYERS
Courtesy Akron Beacon Journal

CRAIG MACINTOSH
Courtesy Minneapolis Star

JERRY ROBINSON
©Cartoonists and Writers Syndicate

THE TERRORISTS ALWAYS AIM
FOR THE LEGS

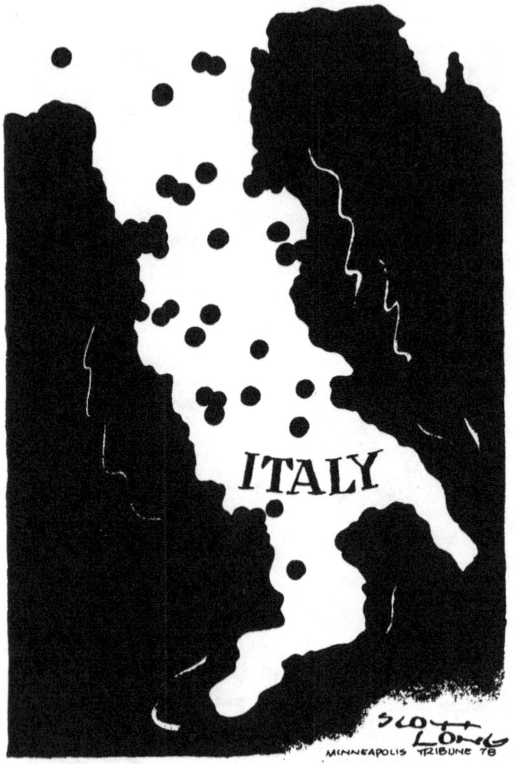
ITALY
MINNEAPOLIS TRIBUNE 78

SCOTT LONG
Courtesy Minneapolis Tribune

ART HENRIKSON
©Paddock Publications

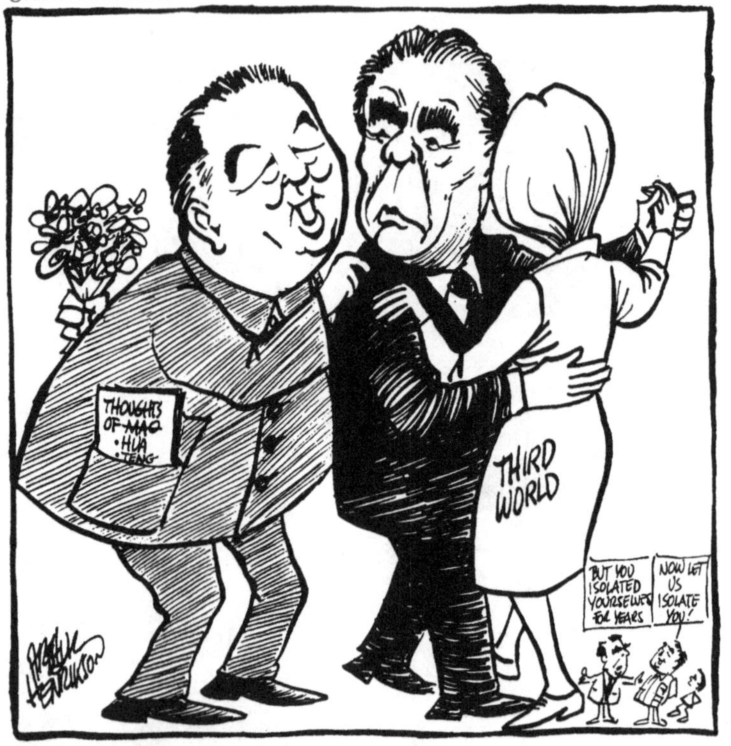
THOUGHTS OF MAO · HUA · TENG
THIRD WORLD
BUT YOU ISOLATED YOURSELVES FOR YEARS
NOW LET US ISOLATE YOU!

A thousand pardons, despicable superpower, I am cutting in!

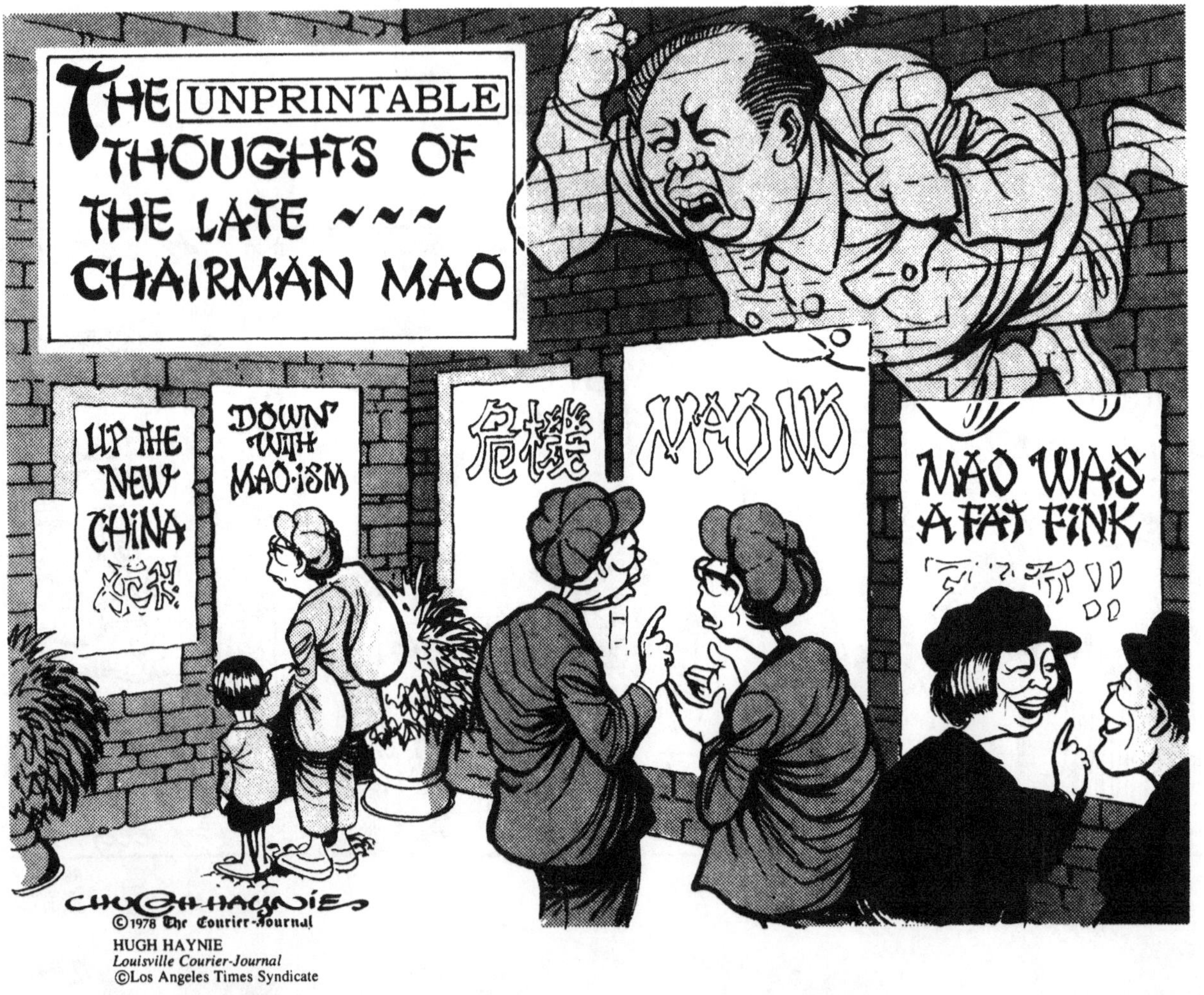
THE UNPRINTABLE THOUGHTS OF THE LATE ~~~ CHAIRMAN MAO
UP THE NEW CHINA
DOWN WITH MAO·ISM
危機
MAO NO
MAO WAS A FAT FINK
©1978 The Courier-Journal

HUGH HAYNIE
Louisville Courier-Journal
©Los Angeles Times Syndicate

Supreme Court Rulings

The U.S. Supreme Court during 1978 tackled a potentially momentous issue, and its historic decision seemed to point in several directions simultaneously. Allan Bakke, a white student, claimed in a suit that the medical school of the University of California had unlawfully denied him admission because of reverse racial discrimination practices. Under an affirmative action policy of the school, a fixed number of spots in each class were allotted to minority students.

In a tight 5-4 decision, the Supreme Court held that race could be a factor in a flexible affirmative action program, but that the University of California's policy of quota system was too rigid.

Several Supreme Court decisions related to freedom of the press gave editors throughout the country cause for concern. The current court seemed to be saying that the press should enjoy no special privileges under the First Amendment. Among the rulings was one decreeing that newspaper offices have no protection against police search—as long as there is a valid search warrant.

"So you demand to call your editors? But, sir, we ARE now your editors!"

HUGH HAYNIE
Louisville Courier-Journal
©Los Angeles Times Syndicate

EVERY MAN'S LOSS

VERN THOMPSON
Courtesy Lawton (Okla.) Constitution

Ah, But I'm Not The Congress

REG MANNING
Courtesy Arizona Republic

S. C. RAWLS
Courtesy Palm Beach Post

'Hey, We're Getting Better!'

TOM ENGELHARDT
Courtesy St. Louis Post-Dispatch

BEWARE THE SERPANT

BERT WHITMAN
Courtesy Phoenix Gazette

73

JOHN CRAWFORD
Courtesy Alabama Journal

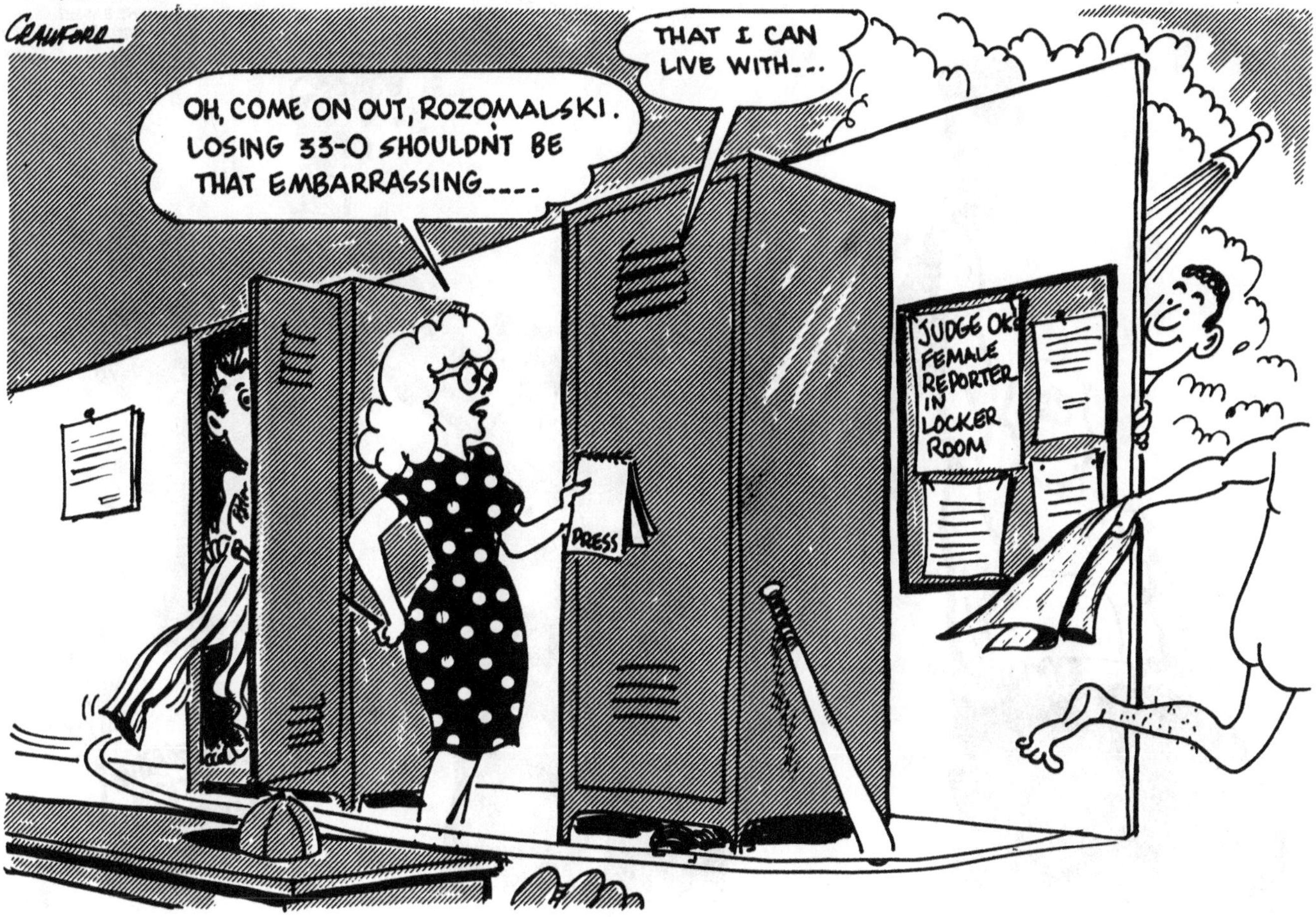
CRAWFORD
OH, COME ON OUT, ROZOMALSKI. LOSING 33-0 SHOULDN'T BE THAT EMBARRASSING....
THAT I CAN LIVE WITH...
JUDGE OKS FEMALE REPORTER IN LOCKER ROOM
PRESS

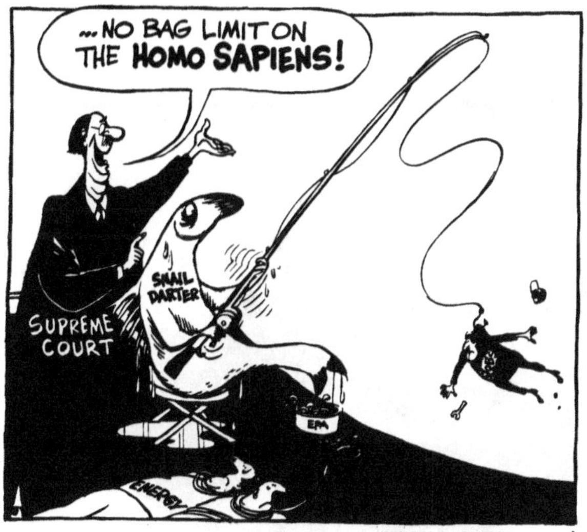
...NO BAG LIMIT ON THE HOMO SAPIENS!
SNAIL DARTER
SUPREME COURT
EPA
ENERGY

JERRY BARNETT
Courtesy Indianapolis News

DAN LYNCH
Courtesy Kansas City Star

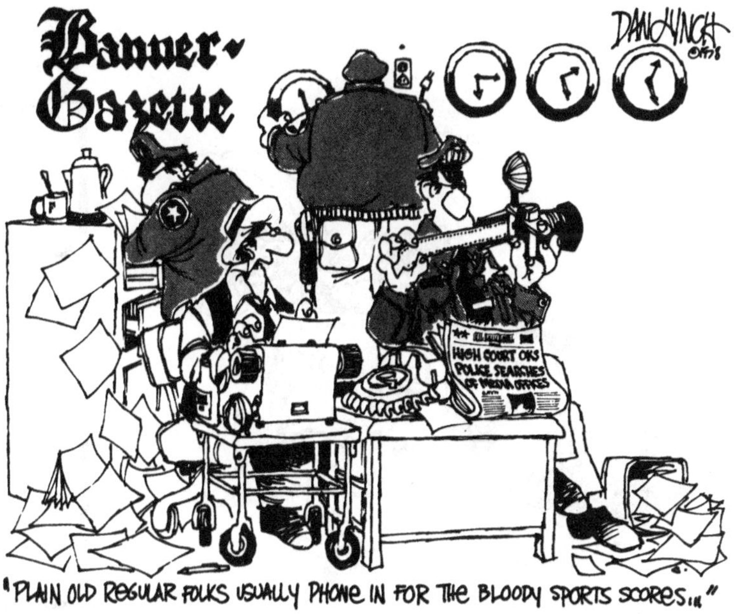
Banner-Gazette
DAN LYNCH ©1978
HIGH COURT OKS POLICE SEARCHES OF MEDIA OFFICES

"PLAIN OLD REGULAR FOLKS USUALLY PHONE IN FOR THE BLOODY SPORTS SCORES..."

GENE BASSET
Courtesy Scripps-Howard Newspapers

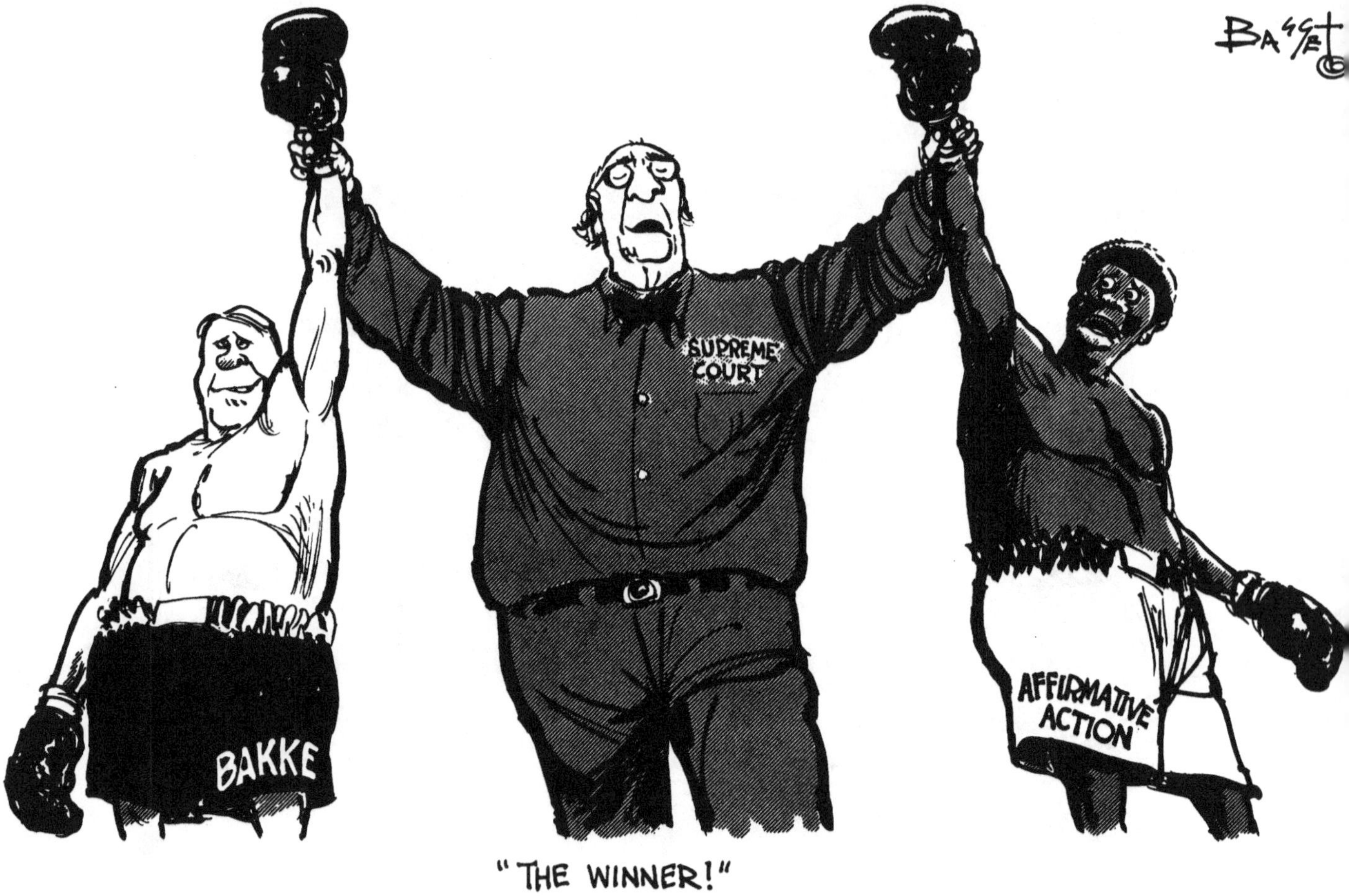
SUPREME COURT
BAKKE
AFFIRMATIVE ACTION
"THE WINNER!"

TOM CURTIS
Courtesy Milwaukee Sentinel

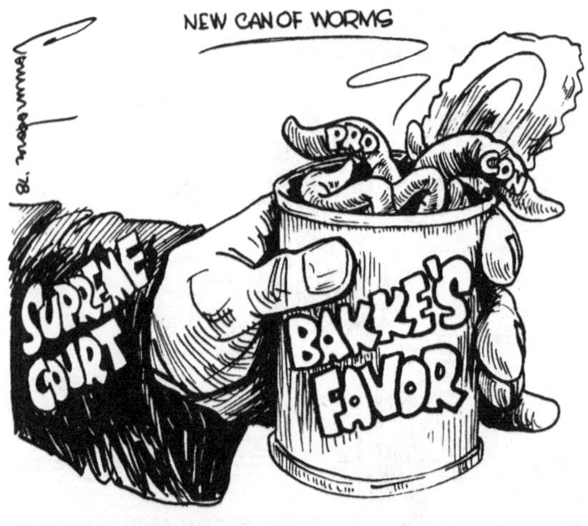
NEW CAN OF WORMS
PRO
CON
SUPREME COURT
BAKKE'S FAVOR

CHESTER COMMODORE
Courtesy Chicago Daily Defender

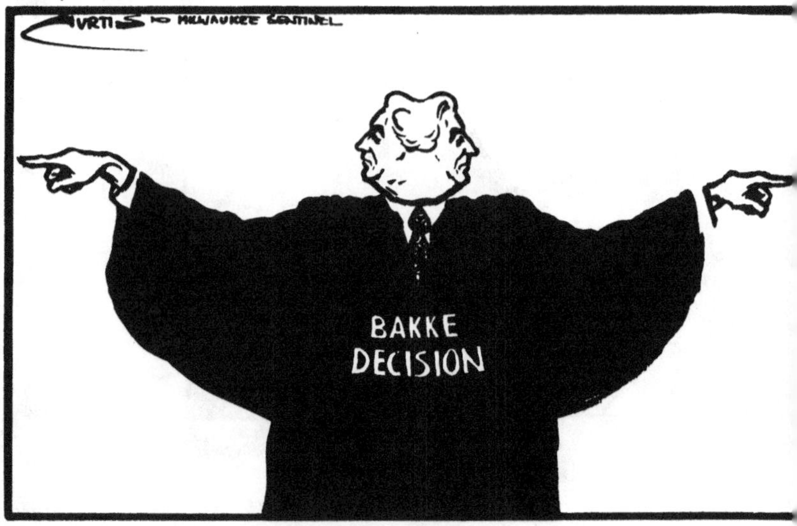
BAKKE DECISION

Affirmative inaction

Koreagate

Testifying before the House Ethics Committee in April, South Korean businessman Tongsun Park acknowledged that he had given some $850,000 to 30 congressmen over a period of several years. Park denied, however, that these cash presents and other gifts were intended to influence U.S. policy toward Korea in any way.

Both houses of Congress and the Justice Department investigated charges of influence-buying for months, but little solid evidence of wrongdoing was turned up. Finally, in a House vote on October 13, three California congressmen were "reprimanded," but not censured, for accepting money from Park. They were Reps. John McFall, Edward Roybal, and Charles Wilson.

A few days later, the Senate Ethics Committee suggested that the Justice Department examine evidence that Sen. Birch Bayh, Democrat of Indiana, or an aide might have broken the law by accepting money while on federal property. The report also charged that the late Sen. John McClellan and the late Sen. Hubert Humphrey's 1972 campaign organization had failed to report contributions from the Korean businessman.

TONGSUN PARK TELLS ALL

GENE BASSET
Courtesy Scripps-Howard Newspapers

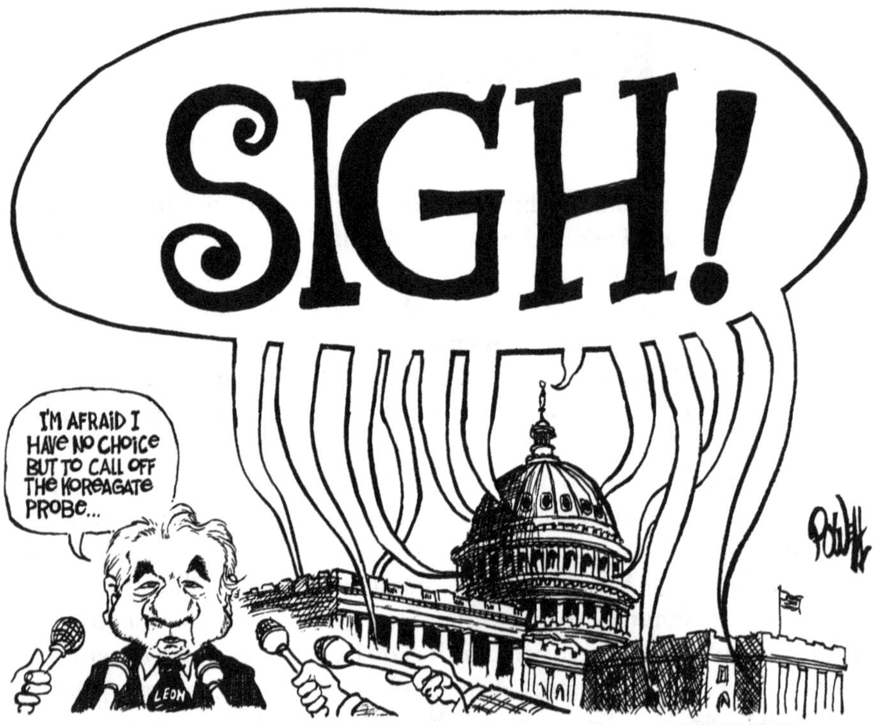
SIGH!
I'M AFRAID I HAVE NO CHOICE BUT TO CALL OFF THE KOREAGATE PROBE...
LEON

DWANE POWELL
Courtesy News and Observer

ED GAMBLE
Courtesy Nashville Banner

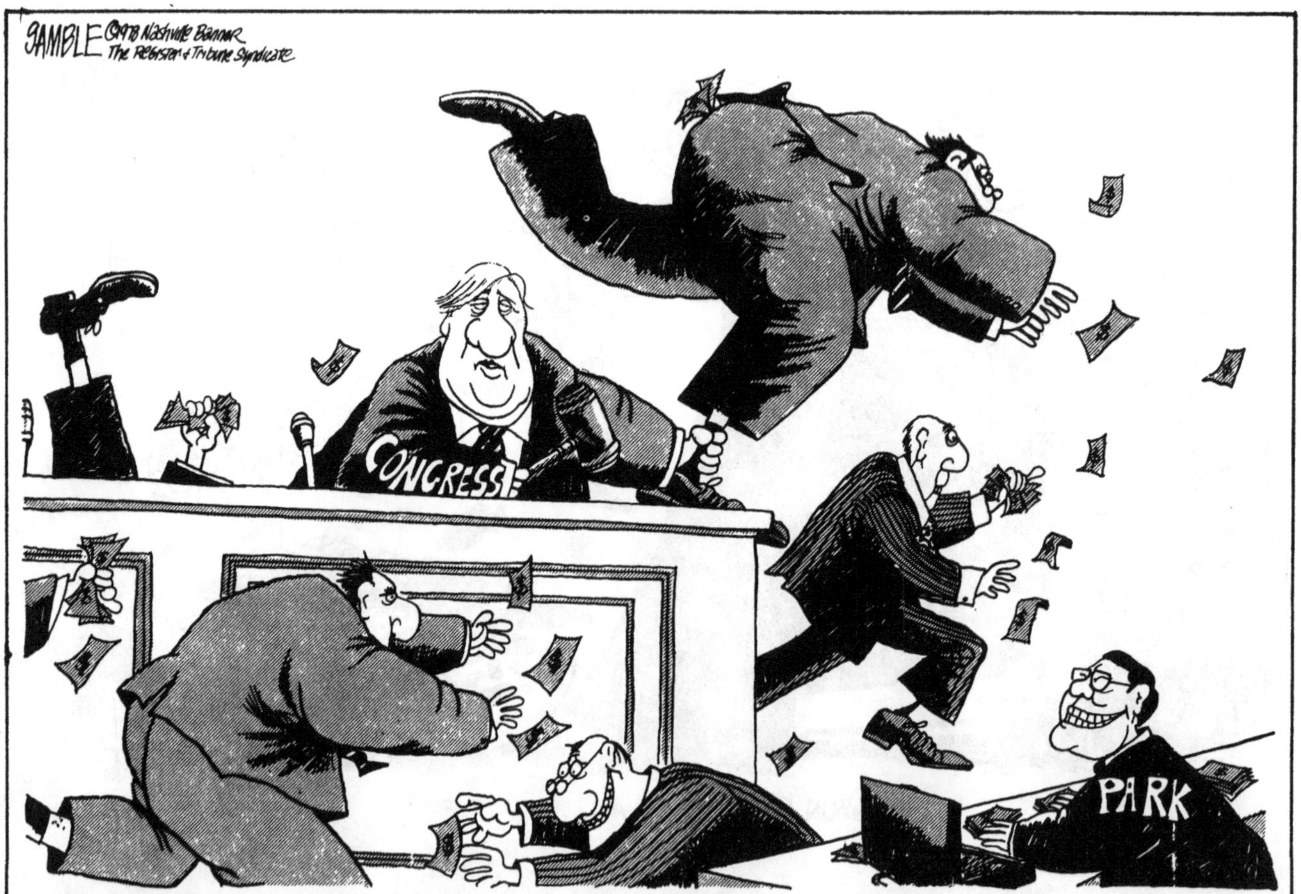
GAMBLE ©1978 Nashville Banner
The Register & Tribune Syndicate
CONGRESS
PARK
"MR. PARK, WOULD YOU REFRAIN FROM THROWING MONEY WHEN A QUESTION IS ASKED? A SIMPLE YES OR NO WOULD SUFFICE!"

ETTA HULME
Courtesy Ft. Worth Star-Telegram

"WELL, ANYWAY, HE SLIPPED AWAY QUIETLY, JUST AS HE LIVED —I THINK HE WOULD HAVE LIKED IT THAT WAY"

DENNIS RENAULT
Courtesy Sacramento Bee

'Sure, I used to play the piano here, but I never suspected anything naughty went on upstairs!'

GUERNSEY LEPELLEY
Courtesy Christian Science Monitor

'Is this where I used to have those lovely picnics?'

FINI$

CONGRESS
KOREAGATE
10-78
THE LAWTON CONSTITUTION

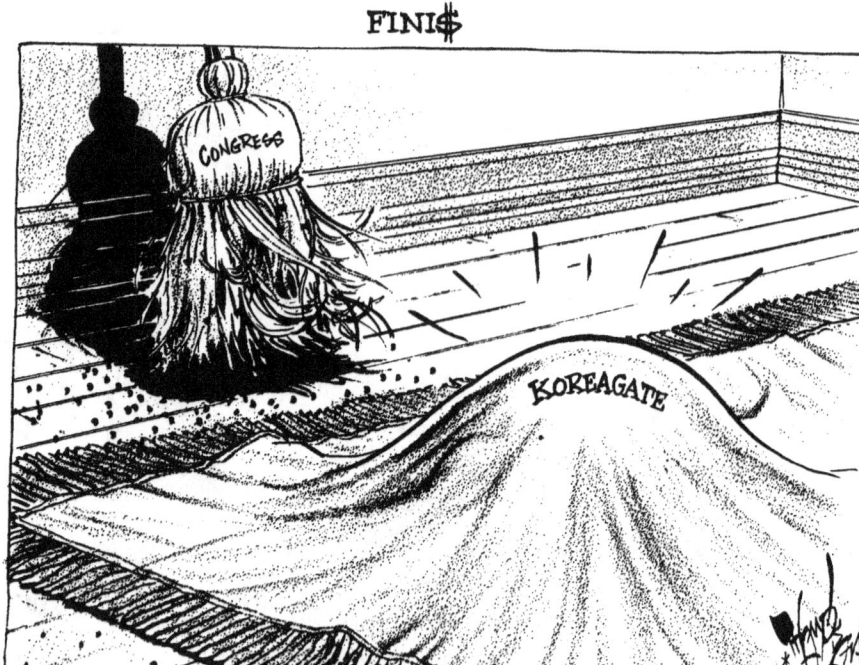

VERN THOMPSON
Courtesy Lawton (Okla.) Constitution

"THE ONE THAT GOT AWAY"

STEIN '78
ROCKY
MTN.
NEWS
KOREAGATE

ED STEIN
Courtesy Rocky Mountain News

The U.S. Congress

Congress came under fire from many directions and sources during 1978. Fraud, corruption, and waste in government were exposed as never before—and much of it reflected badly on Congress itself, which had created the capital's bureaucratic agencies.

Congress was informed that everywhere auditors checked—the Small Business Administration, the Department of Labor, the General Services Administration, the Veterans Administration—criminal acts were uncovered. "All indications are that fraud is a problem of critical proportions," the comptroller general announced, noting that such fraud may total $25 billion, or more than 5 percent of the federal budget.

The lawmakers worked down to the wire in passing a multi-billion-dollar tax cut bill. A diluted energy bill that only faintly resembled President Carter's original proposal also was passed. With a push from Carter, Congress passed laws revamping the civil service—the first such clamp down in a century—and attempting to streamline government. Congress also deregulated the airlines industry, making possible lower air fares.

The lawmakers also took care of themselves, voting to raise their salaries by $12,000 annually, and endorsing continued construction on a new Senate Office Building. The structure, which critics claim eventually will cost $200 million, will be the most expensive federal building ever built.

'Who can explain the tax revolt? Maybe the people have a feeling they're not getting their money's worth or some other emotional reason'

CRAIG MACINTOSH
Courtesy Minneapolis Star

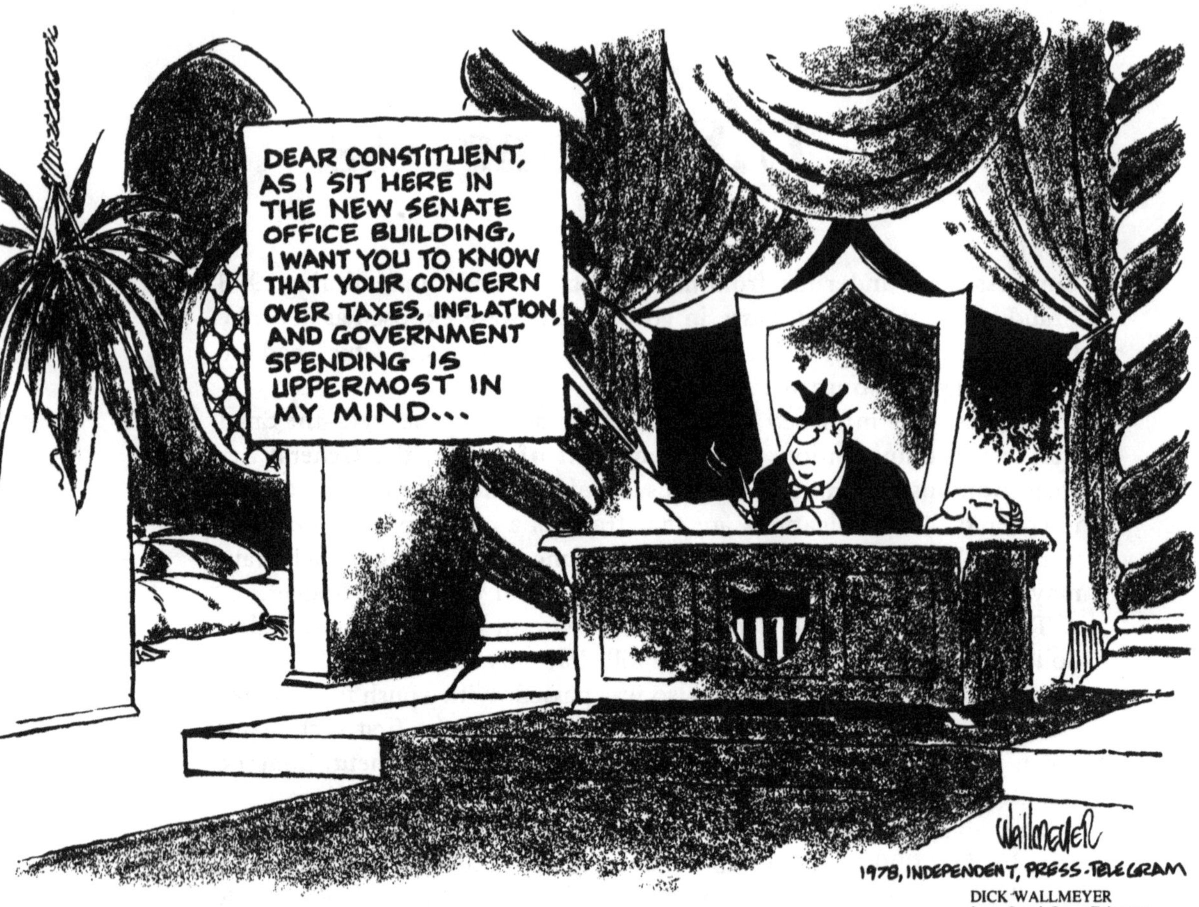
DEAR CONSTITUENT, AS I SIT HERE IN THE NEW SENATE OFFICE BUILDING, I WANT YOU TO KNOW THAT YOUR CONCERN OVER TAXES, INFLATION, AND GOVERNMENT SPENDING IS UPPERMOST IN MY MIND...
Wallmeyer
1978, INDEPENDENT, PRESS-TELEGRAM

DICK WALLMEYER
Long Beach Press-Telegram
©Register and Tribune Syndicate

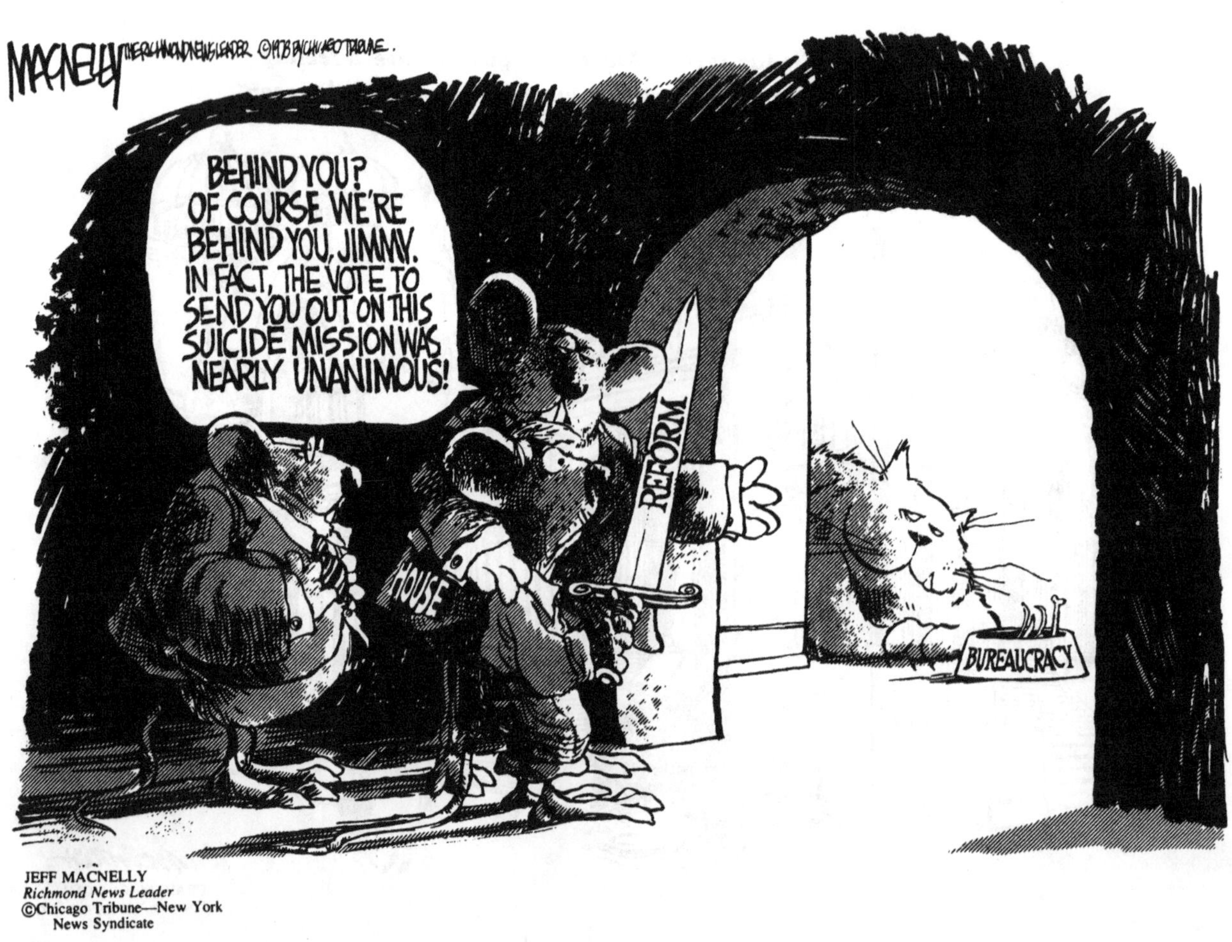
MACNELLY
BEHIND YOU? OF COURSE WE'RE BEHIND YOU, JIMMY. IN FACT, THE VOTE TO SEND YOU OUT ON THIS SUICIDE MISSION WAS NEARLY UNANIMOUS!
REFORM
HOUSE
BUREAUCRACY

JEFF MACNELLY
Richmond News Leader
©Chicago Tribune—New York News Syndicate

CHARLES BISSELL
Courtesy The Tennessean

"Not So Dignified Maybe But It's Our Way To Show Jimmy Can't Lead"

"Look! One of the senators is briefing his staff."

JIM BERRY
©NEA

DICK WRIGHT
Courtesy Providence Journal-Bulletin

Cloning is really nothing new

BOB ARTLEY
Courtesy Worthington (Minn.) Daily Globe

GEORGE FISHER
Courtesy Arkansas Gazette

JON KENNEDY
Courtesy Arkansas Democrat

'Douse that light, you ninny!'

'How's That For The First Tax Cut?'

TOM ENGELHARDT
Courtesy St. Louis Post-Dispatch

CLYDE PETERSON
Courtesy Houston Chronicle

BOB ALEXANDER
Courtesy Lawrence (Mass.) Eagle-Tribune

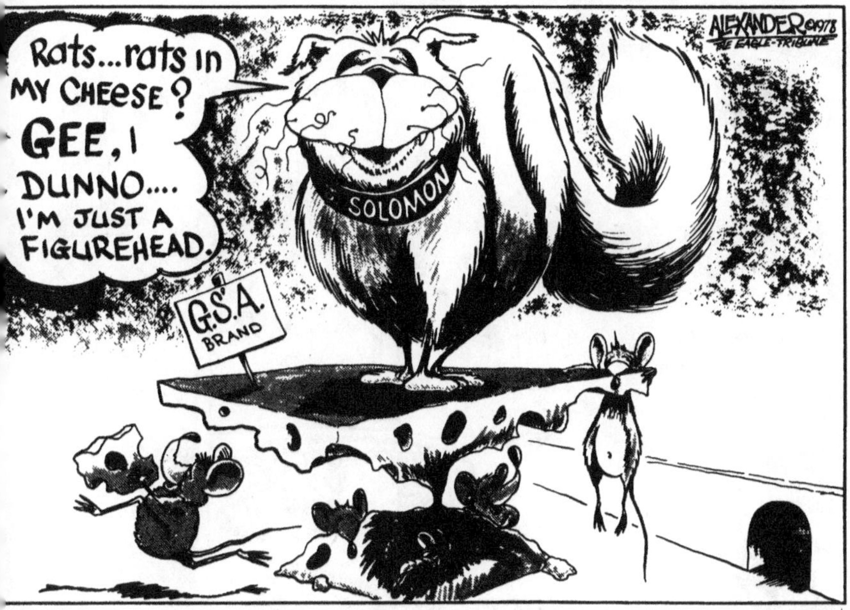
ALEXANDER ©1978 THE EAGLE-TRIBUNE
Rats...rats in MY CHEESE? GEE, I DUNNO.... I'M JUST A FIGUREHEAD.
SOLOMON
G.S.A. BRAND

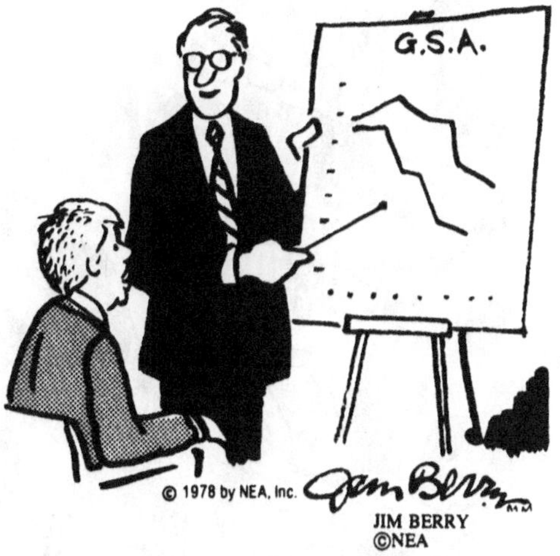
G.S.A.
© 1978 by NEA, Inc.

JIM BERRY
©NEA

" ... And I'm pleased to say that 'massive fraud and kickbacks' is also running behind last week's levels ... "

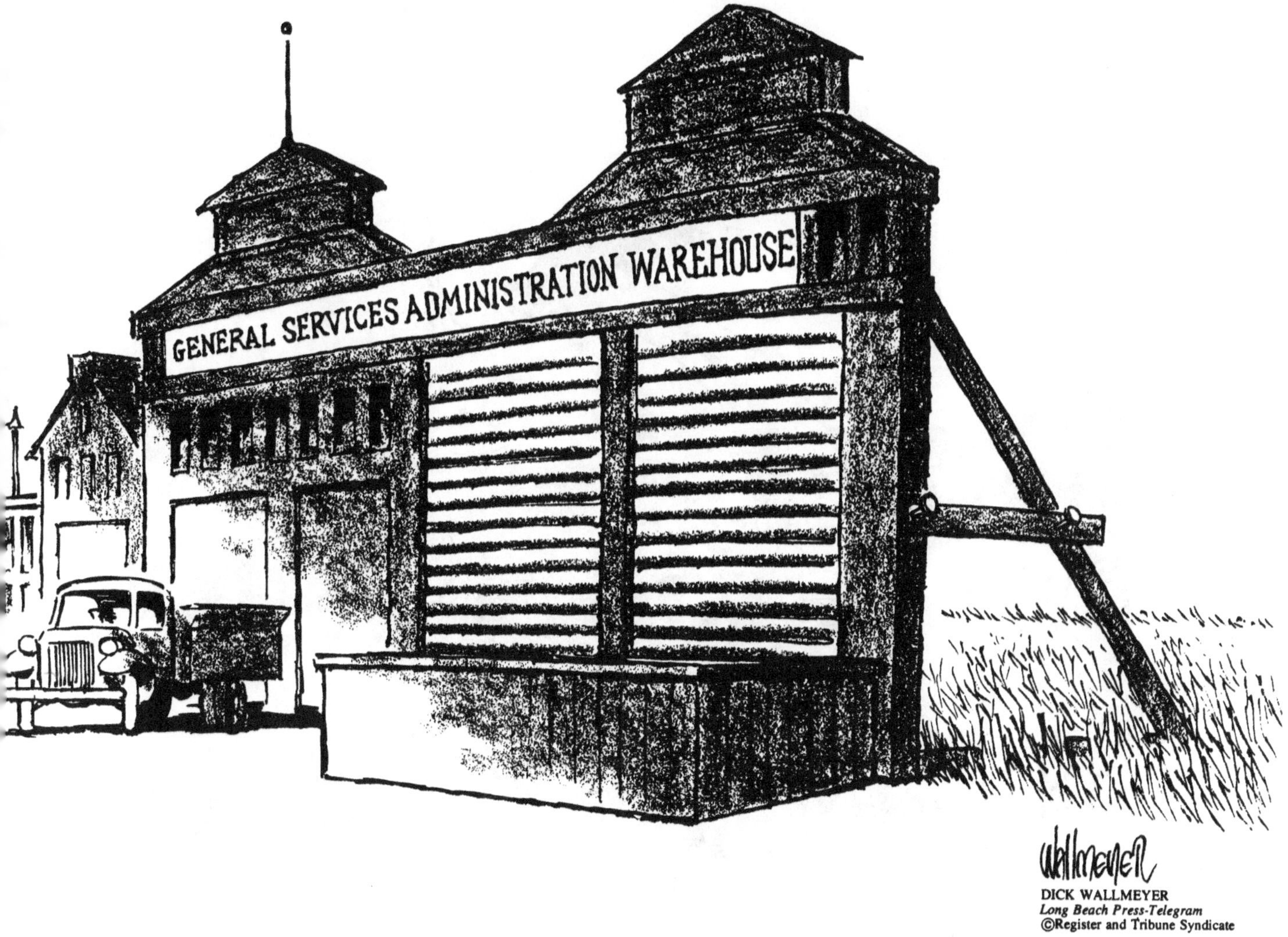
GENERAL SERVICES ADMINISTRATION WAREHOUSE

DICK WALLMEYER
Long Beach Press-Telegram
©Register and Tribune Syndicate

CLYDE PETERSON
Courtesy Houston Chronicle

TOM ENGELHARDT
Courtesy St. Louis Post-Dispatch

'The only responses so far are 1200 hell-no-we-won't-go's with Canadian postmarks'

'Say, How Did You Guess I Finally Signed That Contract For Installing Aluminum Siding On The Washington Monument?'

"I Said That Guy Baker There Heading Out The Channel Has Ruined His Political Chances!"

CHARLES BISSELL
Courtesy The Tennessean

BILL GRAHAM
Courtesy Arkansas Gazette

ED VALTMAN
©Rothco

JIM BORGMAN
Courtesy Cincinnati Enquirer

BILL GARNER
Courtesy Memphis Commercial Appeal

JOHN TREVER
Courtesy Albuquerque Journal

The Soviet Union

American military strategists sounded warnings during the year as the Soviet Union continued to amass a powerful force that could be used in war. Many experts predicted that by 1983 Russia will have achieved an unprecedented strategic advantage over the United States. At that point, it was reasoned, the Soviets would be in a position to threaten the free world, including the U.S., with a knockout attack against our entire missile system. With such a superior capability, they could intervene in any crisis area in the world.

At the same time, Russia was experiencing increased difficulty in its domestic economy, in a growing challenge from Red China, and in strained relations with East European communist states.

The spirit of detente proclaimed so loudly and proudly in 1972 barely remained alive in 1978, thanks to showcase trials of Soviet dissidents such as Yuri Orlov, Alexander Ginsburg, and Anatoly Shcharansky. The three received harsh sentences for allegedly spreading anti-Soviet propaganda and for treason.

RAY OSRIN
Courtesy Cleveland Plain Dealer

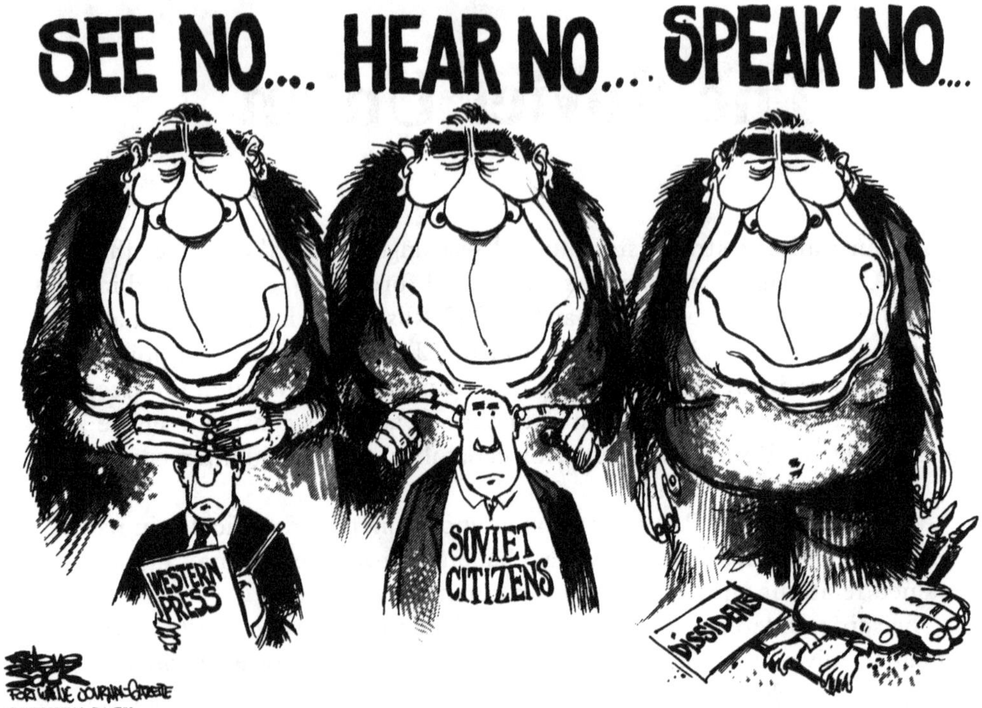
SEE NO.... HEAR NO.... SPEAK NO....
WESTERN PRESS
SOVIET CITIZENS
DISSIDENTS

STEPHEN SACK
Courtesy Ft. Wayne Journal

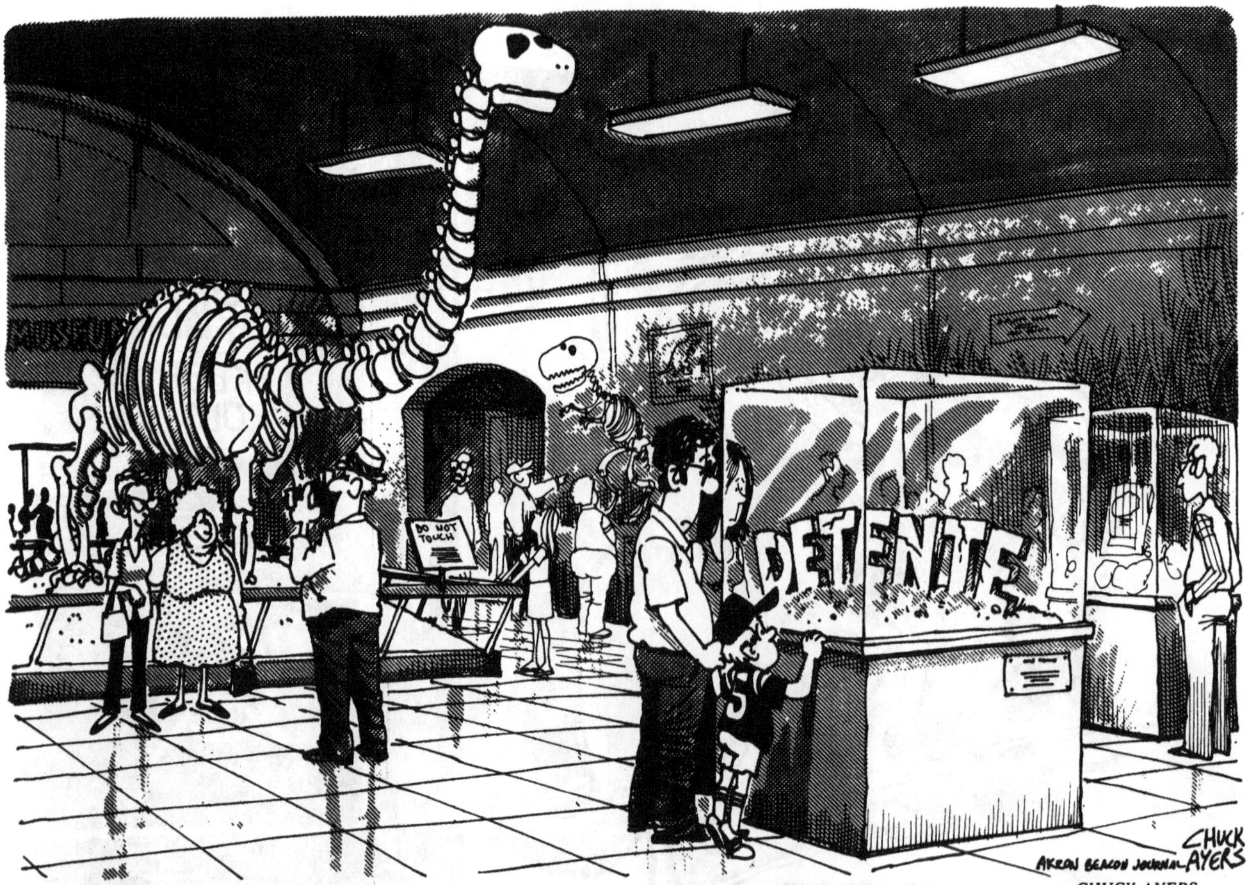
DO NOT TOUCH
DETENTE
CHUCK AYERS
AKRON BEACON JOURNAL

CHUCK AYERS
Courtesy Akron Beacon Journal

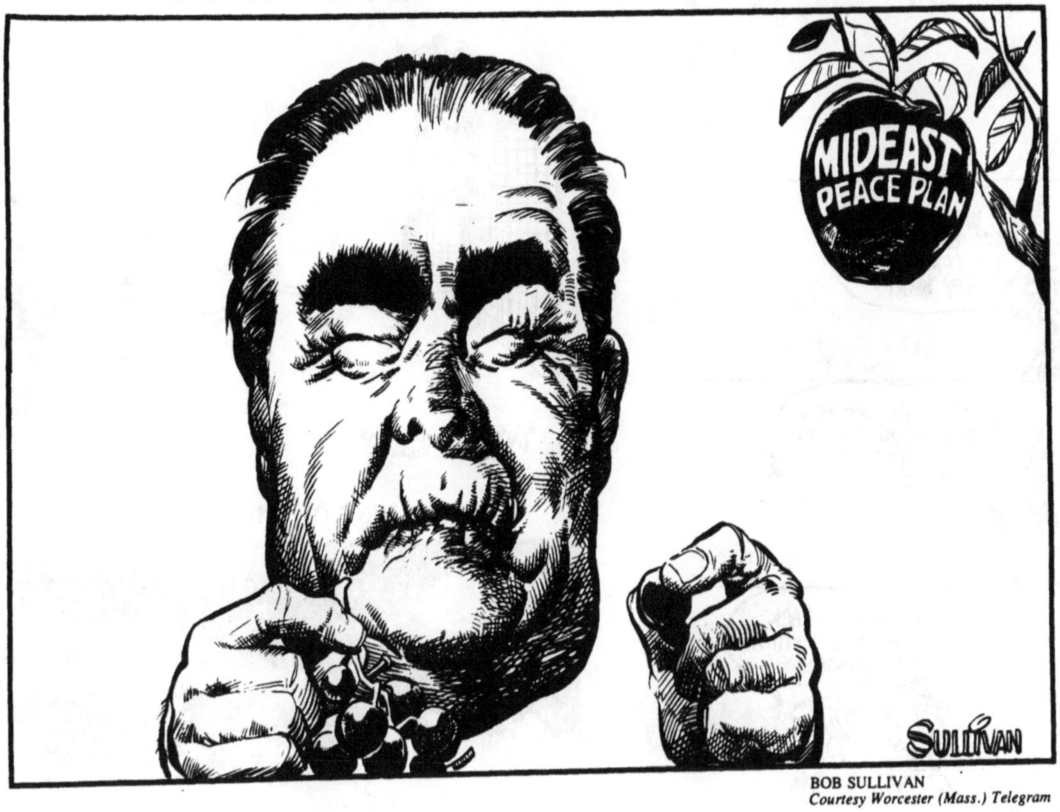
MIDEAST
PEACE PLAN
SULLIVAN

BOB SULLIVAN
Courtesy Worcester (Mass.) Telegram

ED GAMBLE
Courtesy Nashville Banner

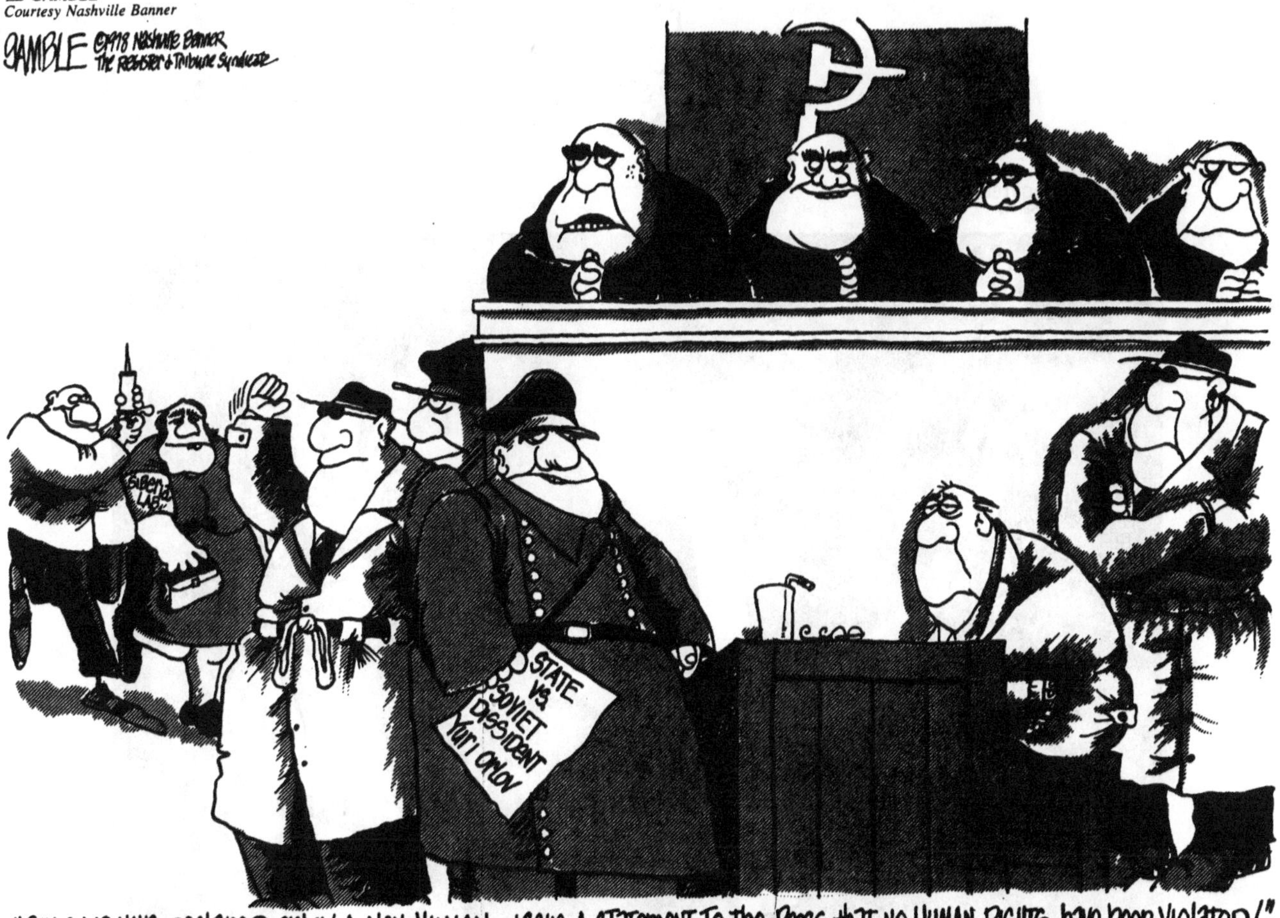
GAMBLE ©1978 Nashville Banner The Register & Tribune Syndicate
STATE VS. SOVIET DISSIDENT YURI ORLOV
"SINCE WE HAVE DECLARED ORLOV A NON-HUMAN.... ISSUE A STATEMENT TO THE PRESS THAT NO HUMAN RIGHTS HAVE BEEN VIOLATED!"

"ALL I KNOW IS HE SAID SOMETHING ABOUT THE 1980 MOSCOW OLYMPICS."

MARK TAYLOR
©Rothco

"WE SHOULD SELL THE RUSSIANS THE COMPUTERS THEY WANT!"

"WHAT THE HELL DO THE RUSSIANS NEED WITH COMPUTERS?"

"TO KEEP TRACK OF THEIR POLITICAL PRISONERS!"

FRANK INTERLANDI
©Los Angeles Times Syndicate

"TRY TO THINK OF THEM AS BARGAINING CHIPS..."

SCOTT LONG
Courtesy Minneapolis Tribune

DOUGLAS BORGSTEDT
©Copley News Service

SHCHARANSKY

"RUSSIAN JUSTICE"

GENE BASSET
Courtesy Scripps-Howard Newspapers

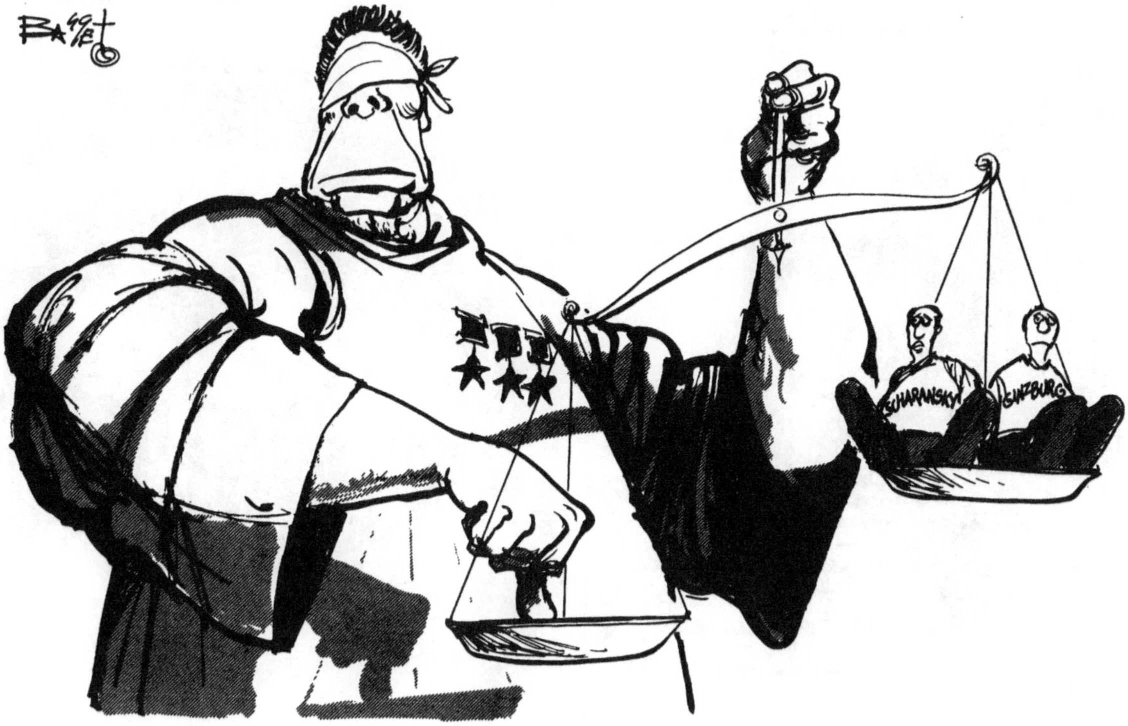
SCHARANSKY
GINZBURG

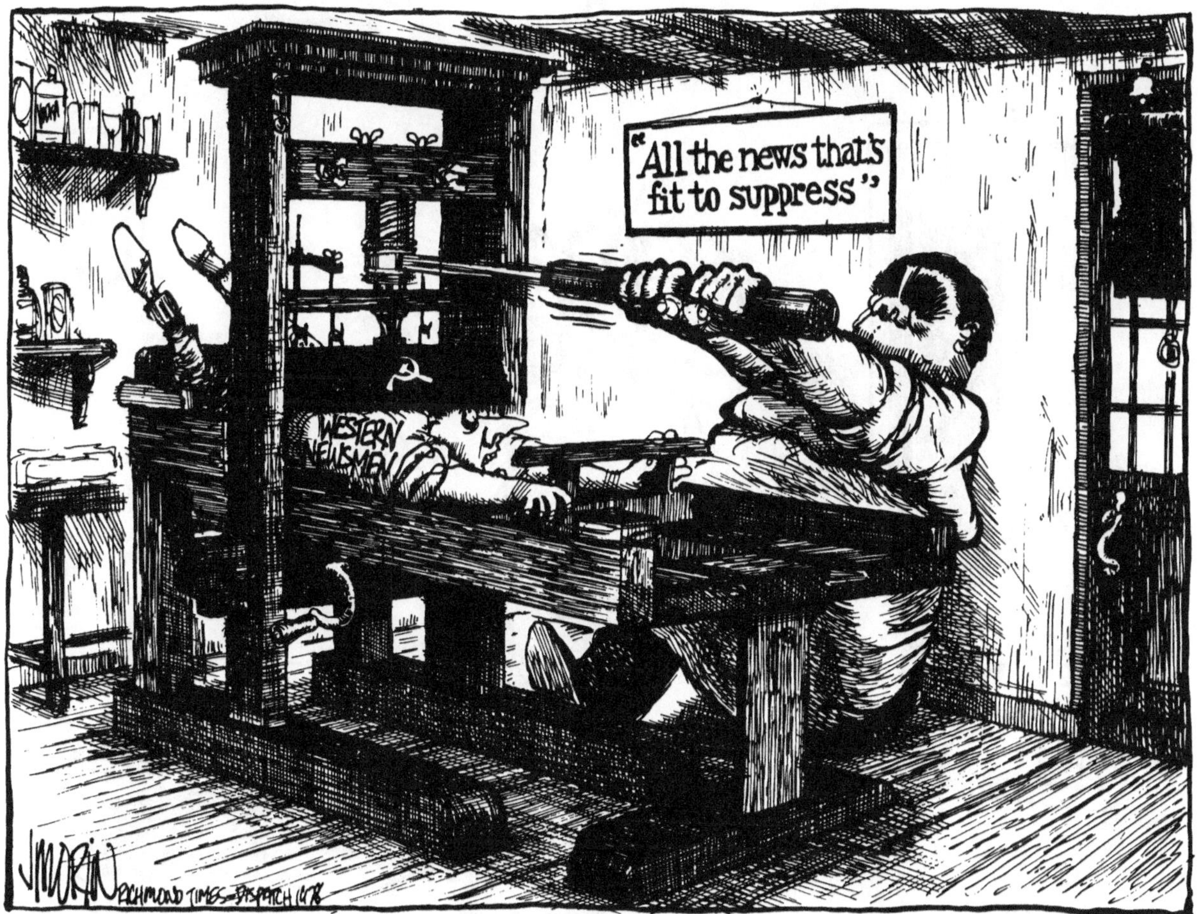
"All the news that's fit to suppress"
WESTERN NEWSMEN
J MORIN RICHMOND TIMES-DISPATCH 1978

JIM MORIN
Courtesy Richmond Times-Dispatch

DICK WALLMEYER
Long Beach Press-Telegram
©Register and Tribune Syndicate

ROGER HARVELL
Courtesy Pine Bluff (Ark.) Commercial

BERT WHITMAN
Courtesy Phoenix Gazette

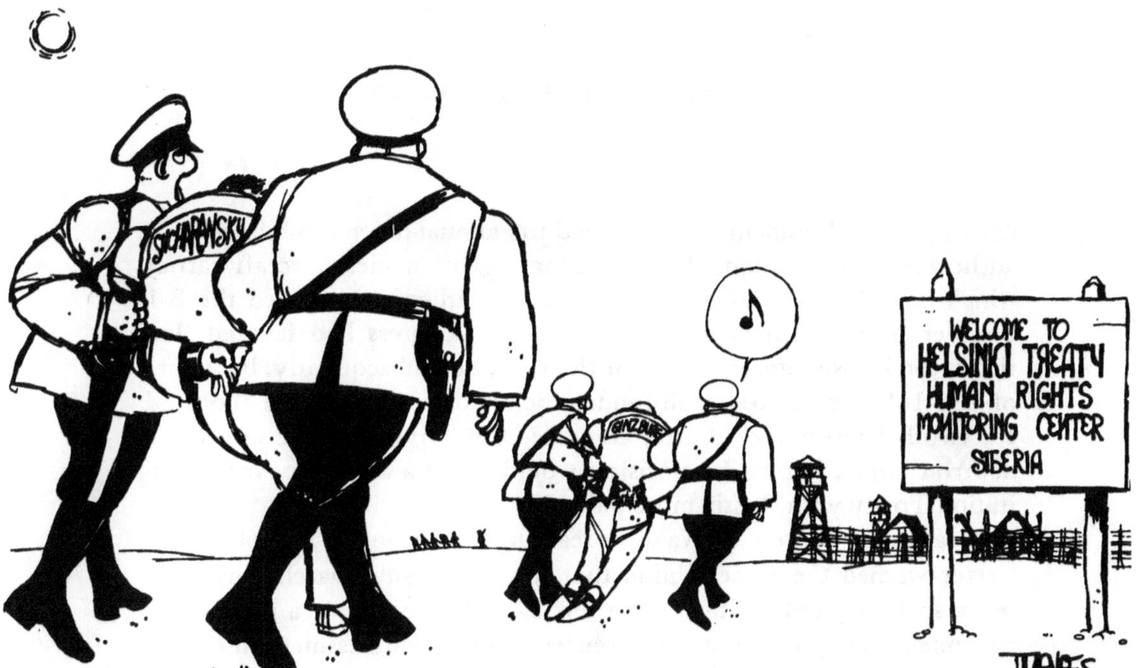

SCHARANSKY
GINZBURG
♪
WELCOME TO
HELSINKI TREATY
HUMAN RIGHTS
MONITORING CENTER
SIBERIA
TMENEES

TIM MENEES
Courtesy Pittsburgh Post-Gazette

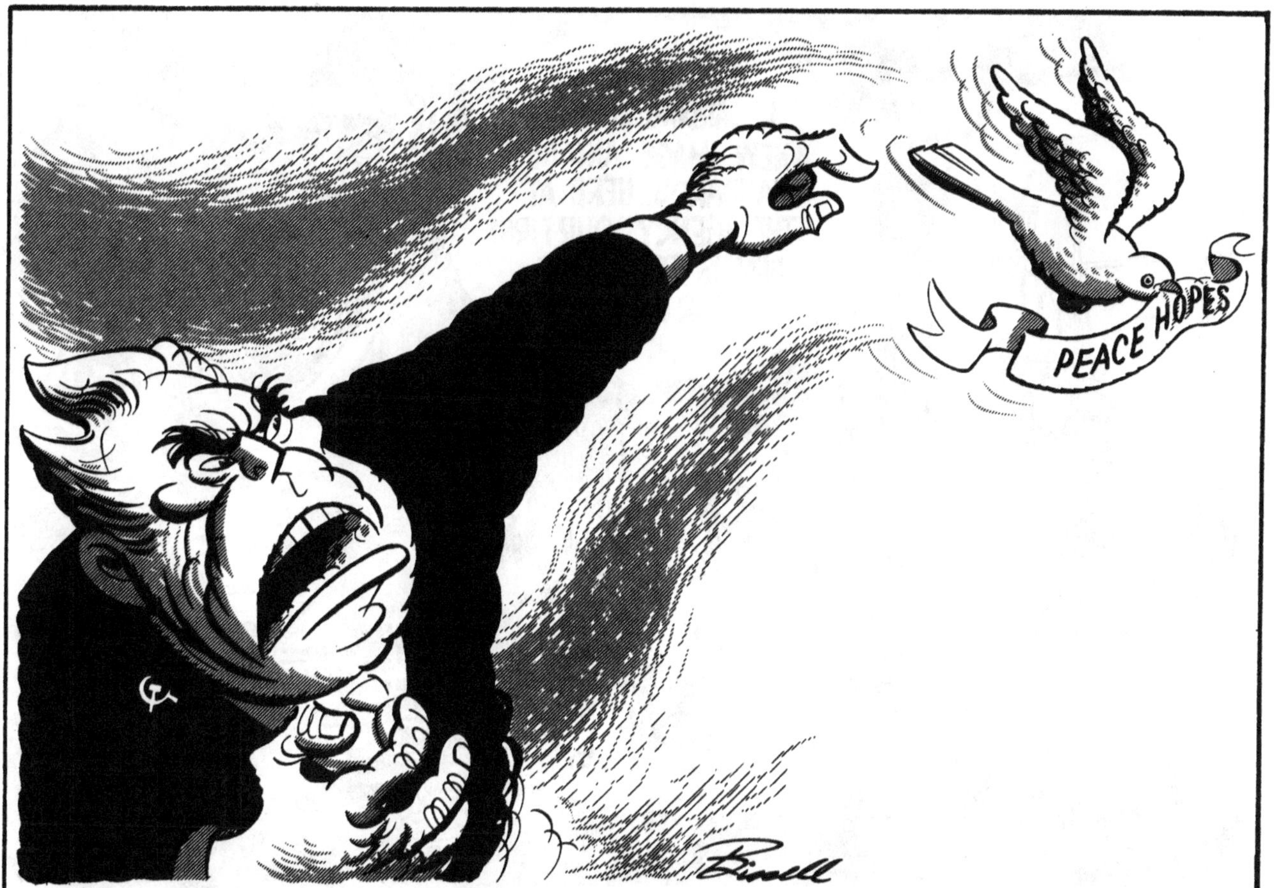

PEACE HOPES
Bissell

"Stop It! It's Ripping Apart The Whole Mideast!"

CHARLES BISSELL
Courtesy The Tennessean

U.S. Defense

On August 17 President Carter vetoed the annual defense bill because it authorized construction of an additional giant nuclear aircraft carrier which would have cost $2 billion. Carter earlier had derailed the B-1 bomber project, which many members of Congress had favored. Initially, the House refused to accept the veto, but subsequently, by a vote of 234-182, agreed to stop all funds which had previously been allocated for two B-1 test models. Carter also ruled out current production of the neutron bomb, hoping his decision would make a Strategic Arms Limitation Treaty with Russia more palatable.

In a major address at Wake Forest University on St. Patrick's Day, Carter warned the Soviet Union that the U.S. would match Soviet defense spending and military force levels—with or without a new SALT agreement. Despite strong differences among congressmen, the long negotiations for a new SALT pact appeared to be nearing successful completion as the year ended.

DICK WRIGHT
Courtesy Providence Journal-Bulletin

BALDY
Courtesy Atlanta Constitution

CLYDE WELLS
Courtesy Augusta (Ga.) Chronicle

LEW HARSH
Courtesy Scranton Times

ROBERT C. DREBELBIS
Courtesy Harrison (Ark.) Daily Times

ED VALTMAN
©Rothco

'PLEASE PASS THE SALT'

"YOU'RE UNDER ARREST FOR HARASSING THAT POOR FELLOW!"

CHARLES BROOKS
Courtesy Birmingham (Ala.) News

"WHAT CAN YOU DO FOR YOUR COUNTRY?"

R. B. RAJSKI
Courtesy Des Plaines (Ill.) Suburban Times

'Is He Your Man Behind the Man?'

JOHN STAMPONE
Courtesy Army Times

"DIOGENES? SAY, YOU'RE ON OUR HIT LIST"

LOU GRANT
Oakland Tribune
©Los Angeles Times Syndicate

Taxpayers' Revolt

A taxpayers' revolt, spawned by weariness of "big government" and spearheaded by Howard Jarvis and Paul Gann in California, spread across the country in 1978. The two leaders wrote and campaigned for a state constitutional amendment, called Proposition 13, that would cut California property taxes by approximately $7 billion. The proposal was approved by a whopping 65 percent of California's voters, thus sending a message eastward that President Carter and Congress heard loudly and clearly.

State officials, including Governor Jerry Brown, opposed the amendment, contending that passage would gravely undermine the state's financial structure. They warned that such a large tax cut would result in intolerable reductions in police and fire protection, school budgets, and such other services as garbage collection. After the votes were tallied, Brown nimbly switched sides, however, admitting that millions could easily be saved by eliminating waste, duplications, and unneeded programs.

The November elections brought home to many politicians the hard fact that most taxpayers are, indeed, out of patience with soaring taxes and waste in government.

JERRY BARNETT
Courtesy Indianapolis News

RAY OSRIN
Courtesy Cleveland Plain Dealer

CHESTER COMMODORE
Courtesy Chicago Daily Defender

"So then Tommy Taxpayer said to the big bully, Godzilla government, 'I am unwilling to pay the bill ...'"

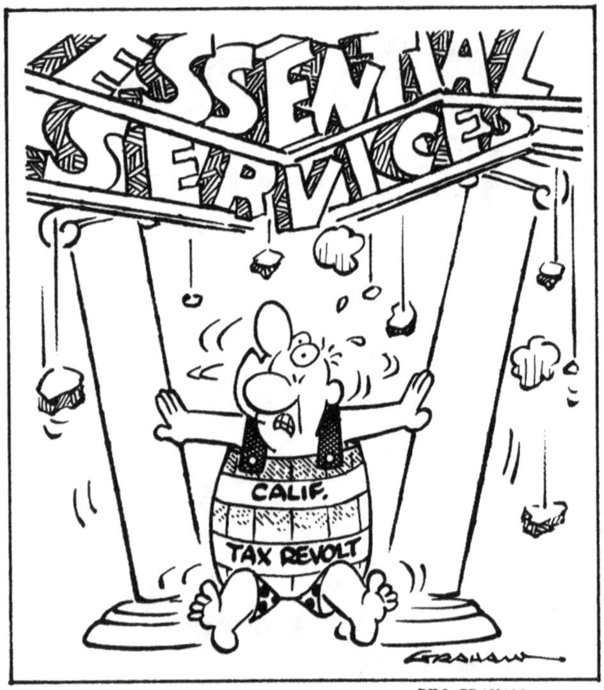
ESSENTIAL SERVICES
CALIF.
TAX REVOLT
GRAHAM

BILL GRAHAM
Courtesy Arkansas Gazette

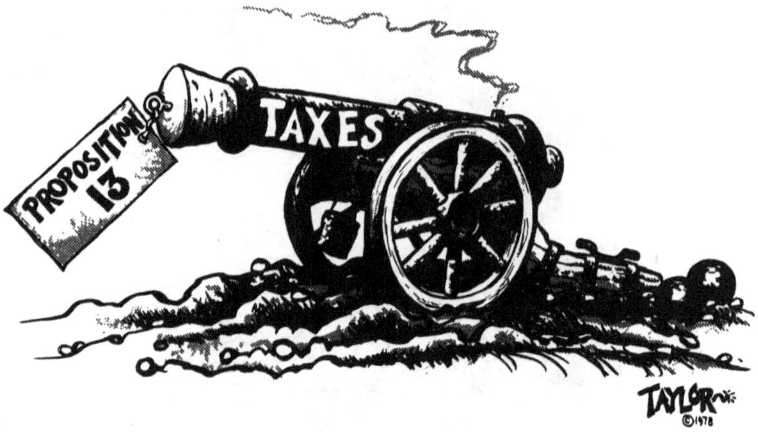
PROPOSITION 13
TAXES
TAYLOR
©1978

THE SPIRIT OF '78

MARK TAYLOR
©Rothco

VIC RUNTZ
Courtesy Bangor Daily News

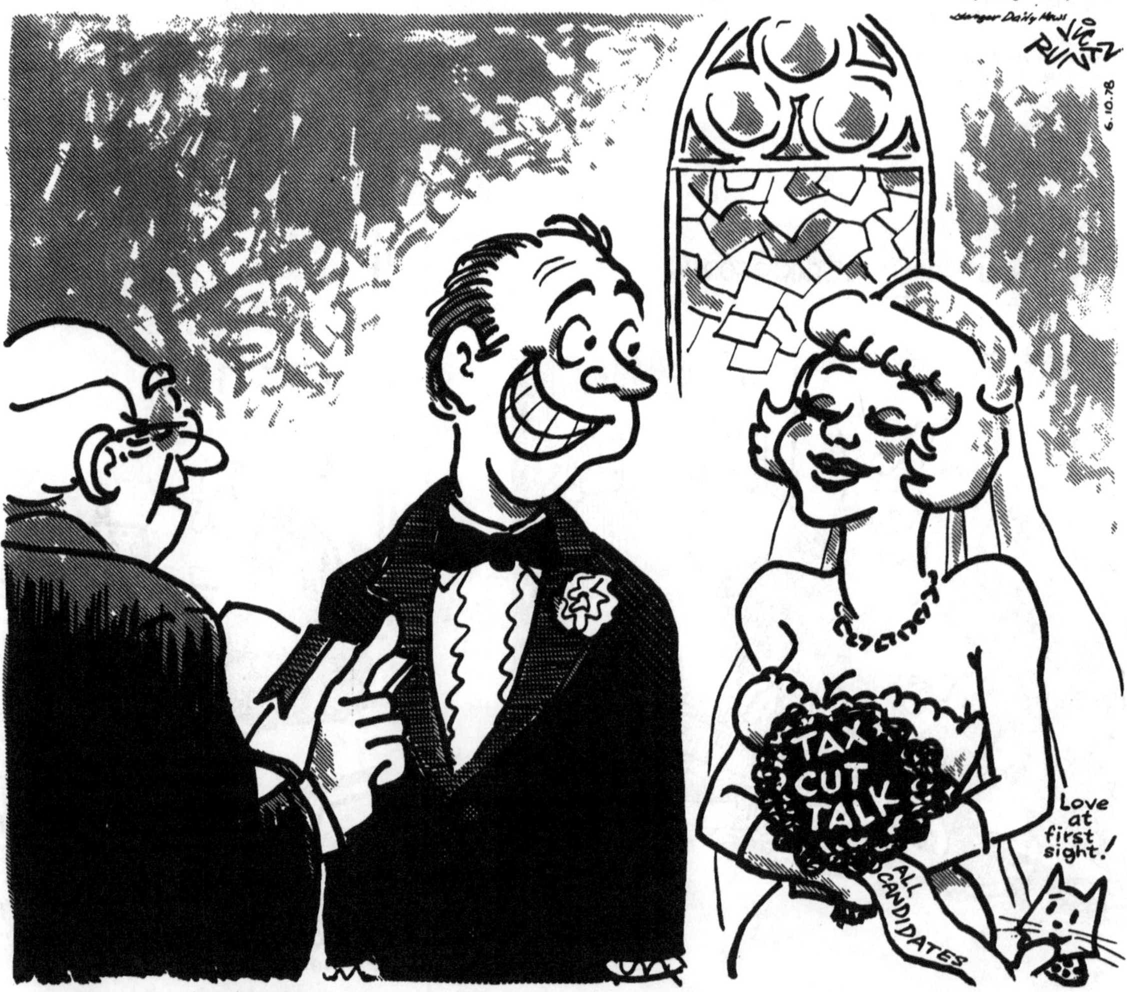
Bangor Daily News
VIC RUNTZ
6.10.78
TAX CUT TALK
ALL CANDIDATES
Love at first sight!

"Do you, John Q. Taxpayer, take . . ."   "DO I EVER!"

LEW HARSH
Courtesy Scranton Times

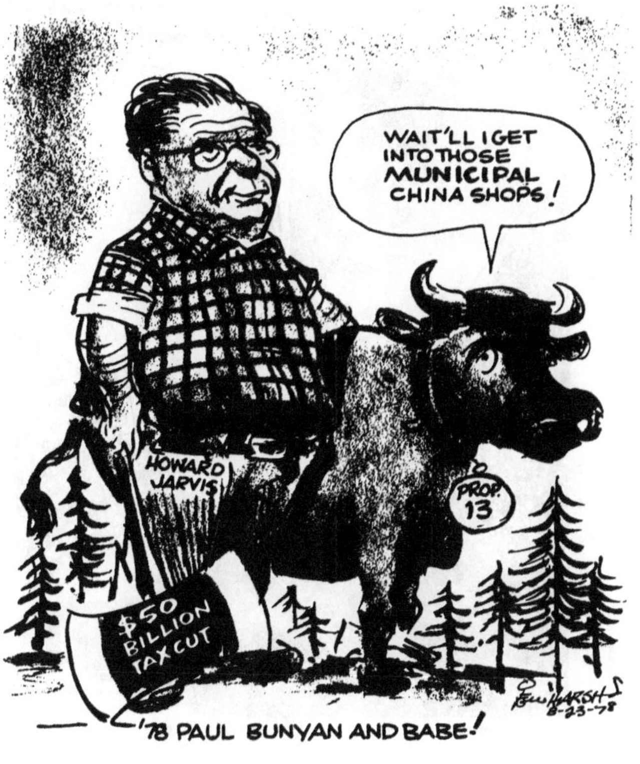
WAIT'LL I GET INTO THOSE MUNICIPAL CHINA SHOPS!
HOWARD JARVIS
PROP. 13
$50 BILLION TAXCUT
'78 PAUL BUNYAN AND BABE!

TIMOTHY ATSEFF
Courtesy Syracuse Herald-Journal

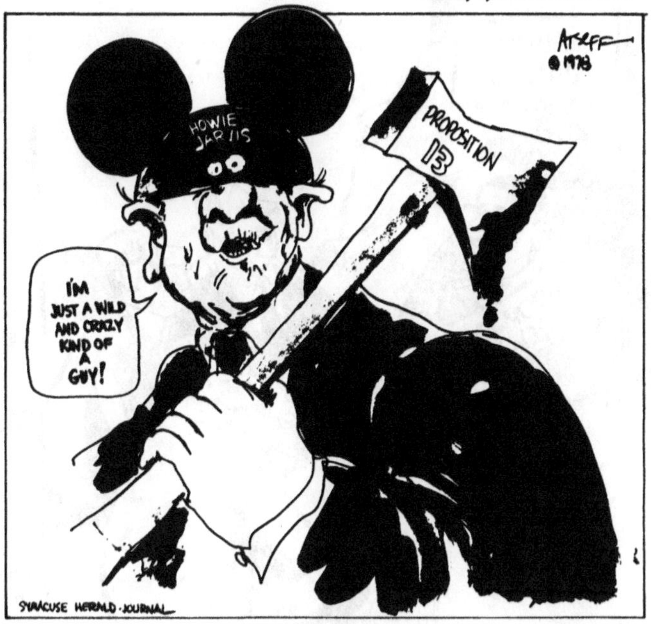
HOWIE JARVIS
PROPOSITION 13
I'M JUST A WILD AND CRAZY KIND OF A GUY!
SYRACUSE HERALD-JOURNAL

MUTINY ON THE "BOUNTY"

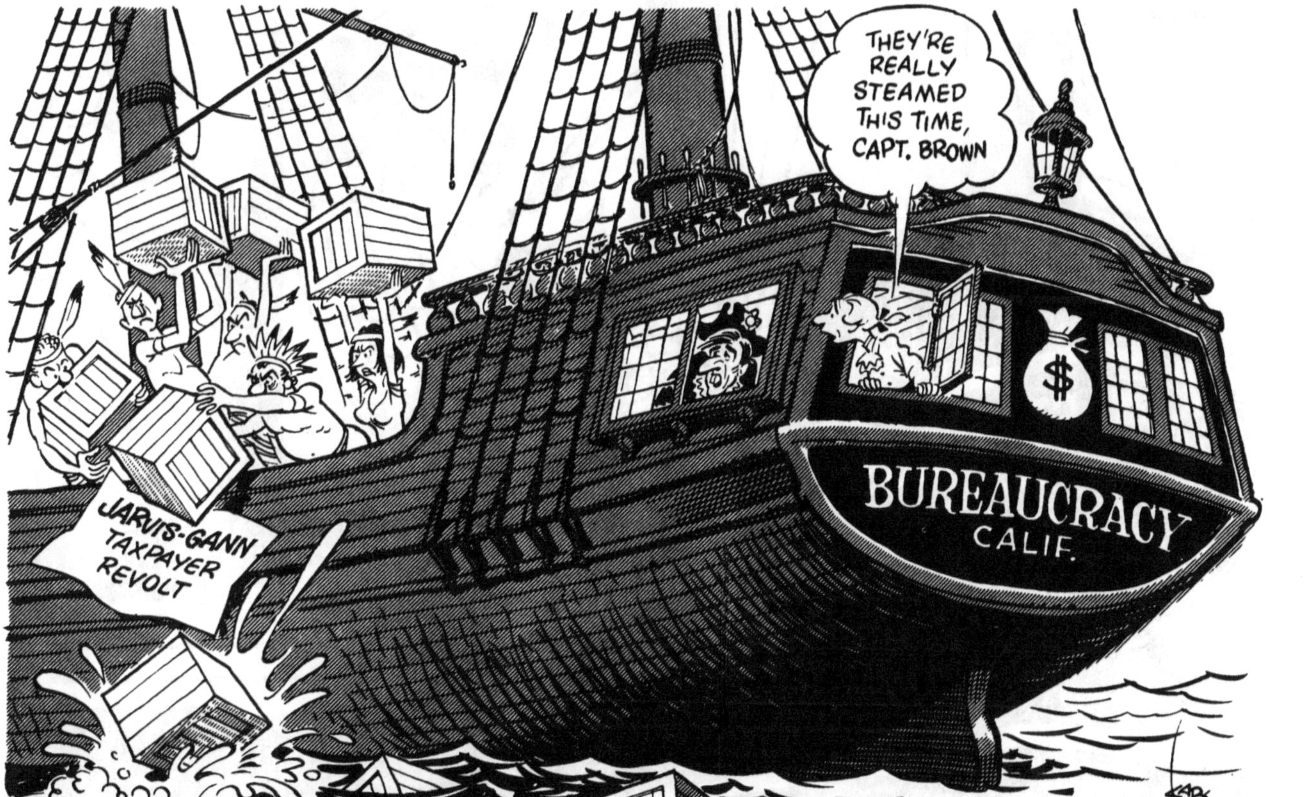
THEY'RE REALLY STEAMED THIS TIME, CAPT. BROWN
$
BUREAUCRACY
CALIF.
JARVIS-GANN TAXPAYER REVOLT

KARL HUBENTHAL
Courtesy Los Angeles Herald-Examiner

TOM FLANNERY
Courtesy Baltimore Sun

JACK McLEOD
Courtesy Buffalo Evening News

"Tell us, Master, What Is The Secret of Re-election?"

'...AND I TELL YOU I HEAR ANOTHER PARADE...'

JIMMY MARGULIES
©Rothco Cartoons

"NEEDY WOMEN AND CHILDREN FIRST!"

PHIL BISSELL
*Courtesy Salem (Mass.)
Evening News*

ED ASHLEY
Courtesy Toledo Blade

BILL DAY
Courtesy Oakland Press

BOB ENGLEHART
Courtesy Dayton Journal Herald

PAUL SZEP
Courtesy Boston Globe

THE HOWARD JARVIS NEUTRON BOMB ... WIPES OUT PEOPLE BUT SAVES THEIR PROPERTY

LOU ERICKSON
Courtesy Atlanta Journal

JIM PALMER
Courtesy Dallas News

Richard Nixon

Former president Richard Nixon emerged from his self-imposed exile at San Clemente to speak at the dedication of a $2.6 million federally financed county recreation center in Hyden, Kentucky on July 2. Nixon addressed a supportive crowd of some 6,000 and warned against communist subversion.

Nixon later received a warm reception at Gulfport, Mississippi on November 11 when he participated in the observance of Veteran's Day at the Gulf Coast Coliseum. Mississippi's retiring senator, John Eastland, thanked him for his help during Hurricane Camille in 1969 while Nixon was president.

After Thanksgiving, Nixon flew to Paris where he appeared on a French public affairs television program. He also made a brief appearance in England where he was greeted by egg-tossing hecklers.

"You've Got Richard Nixon To Kick Around Again!"

JERRY DOYLE
Courtesy Philadelphia Daily News

LOU GRANT
Oakland Tribune
©Los Angeles Times Syndicate

FAKIR

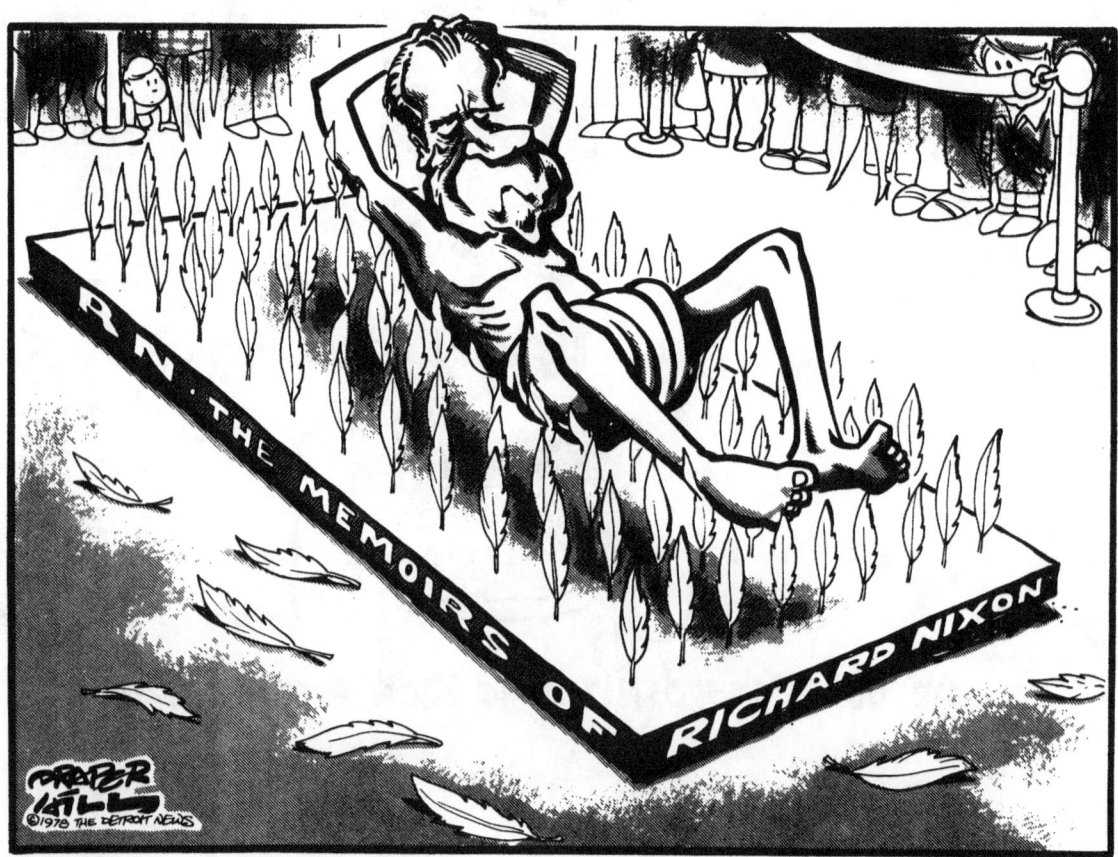

DRAPER HILL
Courtesy Detroit News

ROB LAWLOR
Courtesy Philadelphia Daily News

GEORGE FISHER
Courtesy Arkansas Gazette

BOB TAYLOR
Courtesy Dallas Times Herald

Africa

The Soviet Union and Cuba involved themselves more deeply in African affairs during 1978. The U.S. seemed perplexed and puzzled over how it should react to growing Soviet and Cuban adventurism.

American diplomats moved quietly to limit Soviet influence in Southern Africa. Tensions were reduced between Angola and Zaire and acceptance of a Western-sponsored plan for Namibian independence was sought. The U.S. and Great Britain were anxious to find swift and viable solutions to the conflicts in Namibia (Southwest Africa) and Rhodesia in order to avoid Russian and Cuban intervention on a large scale.

Prime Minister Johannes Vorster resigned on September 20 as the leader of South Africa's National Party ruling government. His successor was Pieter Botha, former minister of defense.

United Nations representative Andrew Young continued his outspoken comments on such topics as African affairs and the plight of blacks in America. Commenting on the trials of Soviet dissidents, Young told reporters in July that "there are hundreds, perhaps thousands, of political prisoners" in the United States.

TOM FLANNERY
Courtesy Baltimore Sun

The Disabled Vet

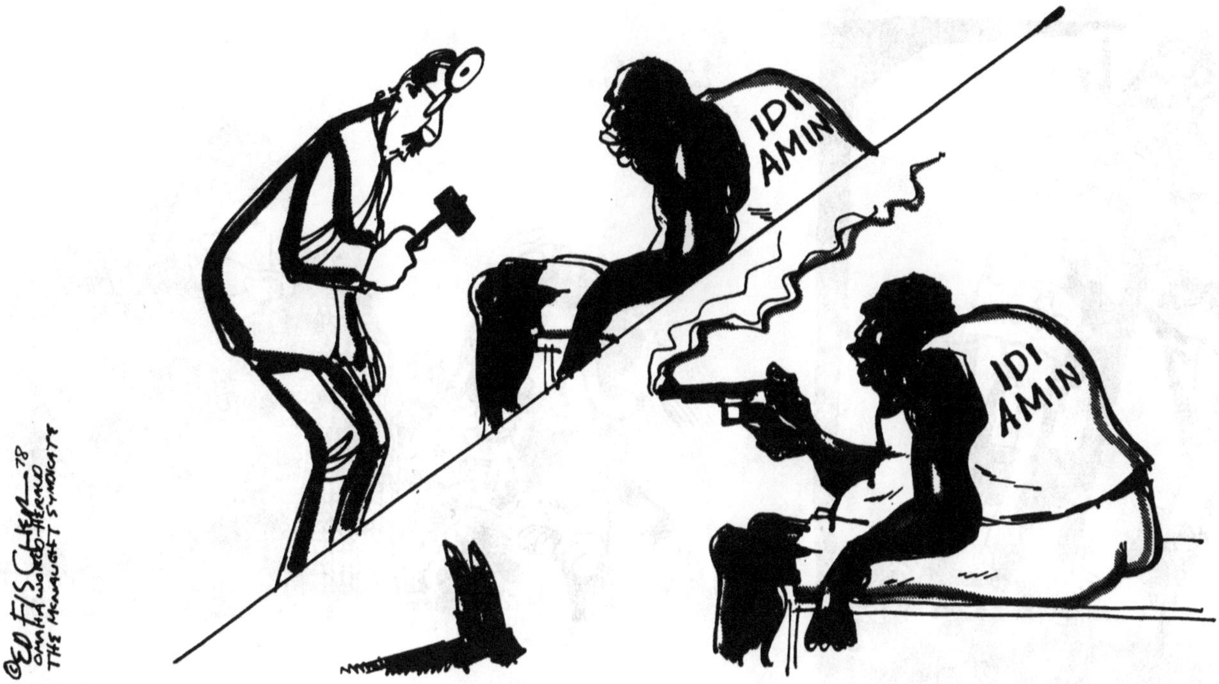
IDI AMIN
IDI AMIN
©ED FISCHER '78 OMAHA WORLD-HERALD THE McNAUGHT SYNDICATE

ED FISCHER
Courtesy Omaha World-Herald

HY ROSEN
Courtesy Albany Times-Union

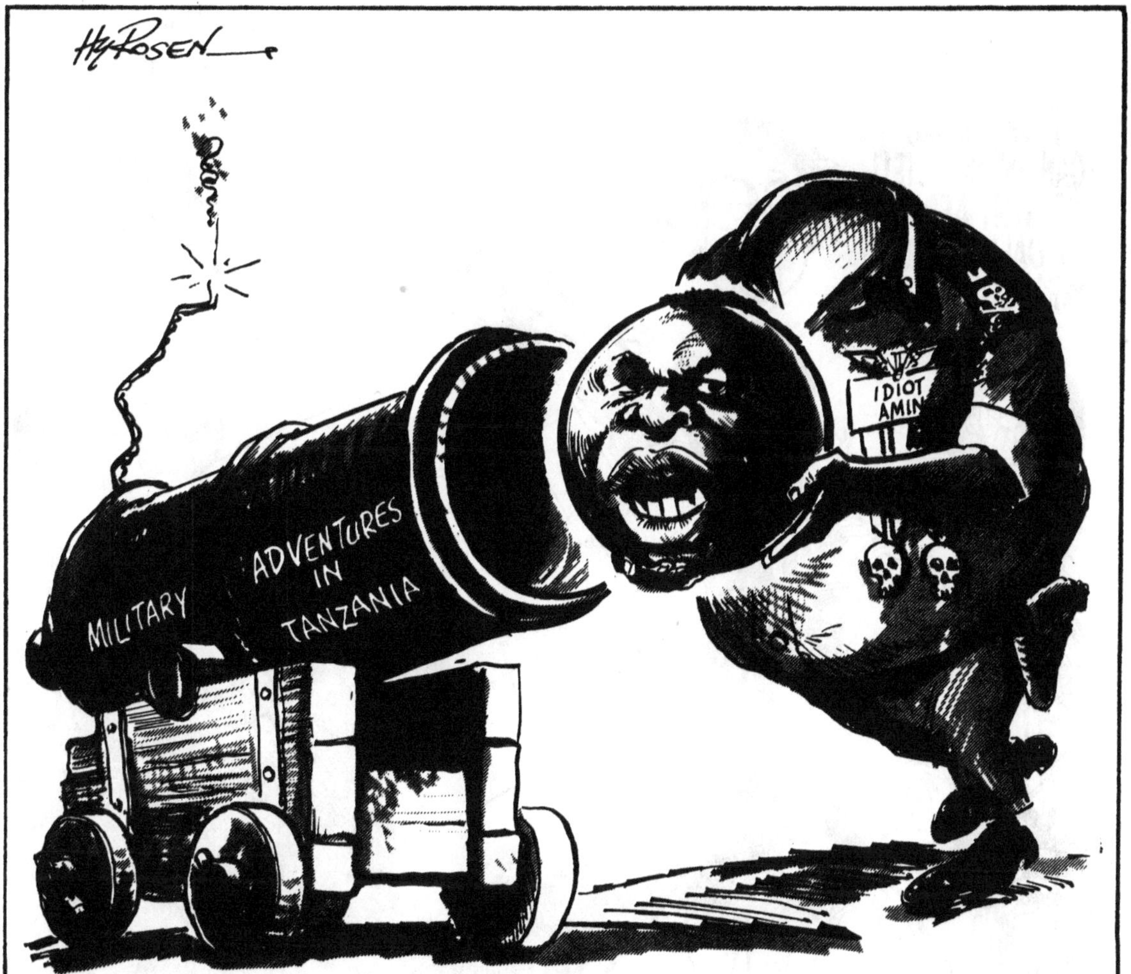
HY ROSEN
MILITARY ADVENTURES IN TANZANIA
IDIOT AMIN

FRANK EVERS
Courtesy N. Y. Daily News

S. C. RAWLS
Courtesy Palm Beach Post

BILL DE ORE
Courtesy Dallas Morning News

ED ULUSCHAK
Courtesy Edmonton (Can.) Journal

REINS OF POWER

VIC CANTONE
Courtesy N.Y. Daily News

JERRY ROBINSON
©Cartoonists and Writers Snydicate

Energy

Iran, one of the world's richest countries in terms of oil reserves, remained the center of internal strife and turmoil throughout the year. Civilian demonstrations against the ruling Shah and his government spawned widespread violence and led to a crippling strike in the country's oil industry.

As oil prices remained high, the world's coal production continued upward. Despite a lengthy coal strike in the U.S., some 3.5 billion tons were mined.

World crude oil output was estimated at about 23,000 million barrels, about 5 percent above the 1977 level. The Soviet Union remained the leading producer, followed by the U.S. and Saudi Arabia. Worldwide production of natural gas was estimated at about 53,000 billion cubic feet, up 4 percent from the previous year. The leading producers were the U.S., Russia, and Canada, in that order.

A growing demand for energy, particularly for reasonably priced energy, spurred nuclear plant development. Opposition by environmental groups continued to be vigorous and loud. More attention was forced on solar energy as a source of power.

Late in the year the Organization of Petroleum Exporting Countries (OPEC) announced a 10 percent increase in the price of oil over the next 18 months.

JEFF MACNELLY
Richmond News Leader
©Chicago Tribune—New York News Syndicate

BILL GARNER
Courtesy Memphis Commercial Appeal

HECTOR VALDES
Courtesy Villa Olympica

JERRY DOYLE
Courtesy Philadelphia Daily News

CHARLES BISSELL
Courtesy The Tennessean

"Well, I Guess It's Better To Light A Candle Than Curse The Darkness"

JACK GOLD
Courtesy Kentucky Post

JIM MORIN
Courtesy Richmond Times-Dispatch

DRAPER HILL
Courtesy Detroit News

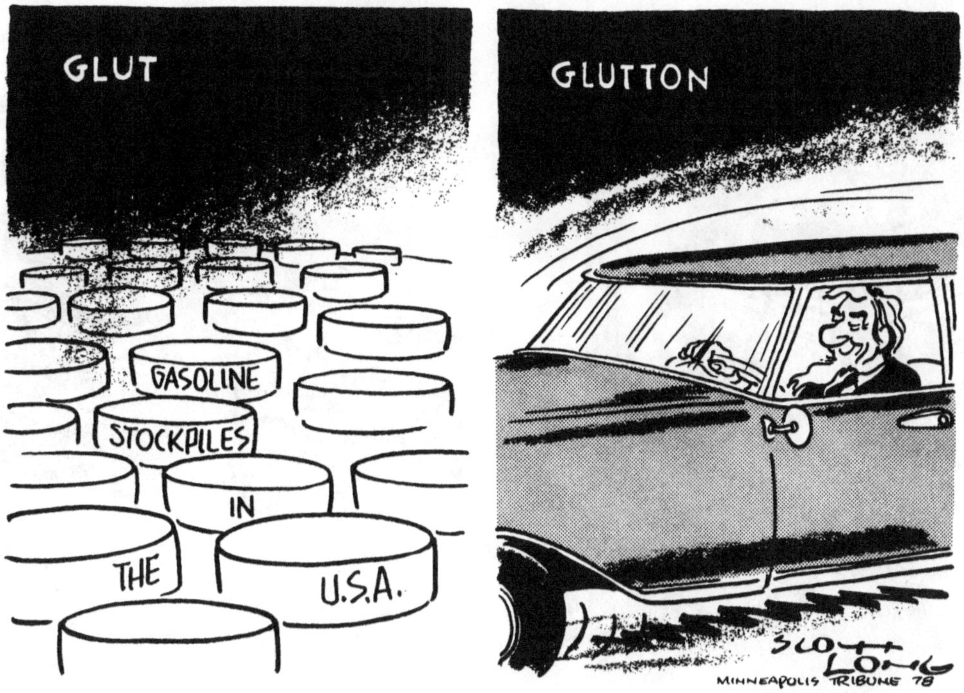
GLUT
GASOLINE
STOCKPILES
IN
THE
U.S.A.
GLUTTON
SCOTT LONG
MINNEAPOLIS TRIBUNE 78

SCOTT LONG
Courtesy Minneapolis Tribune

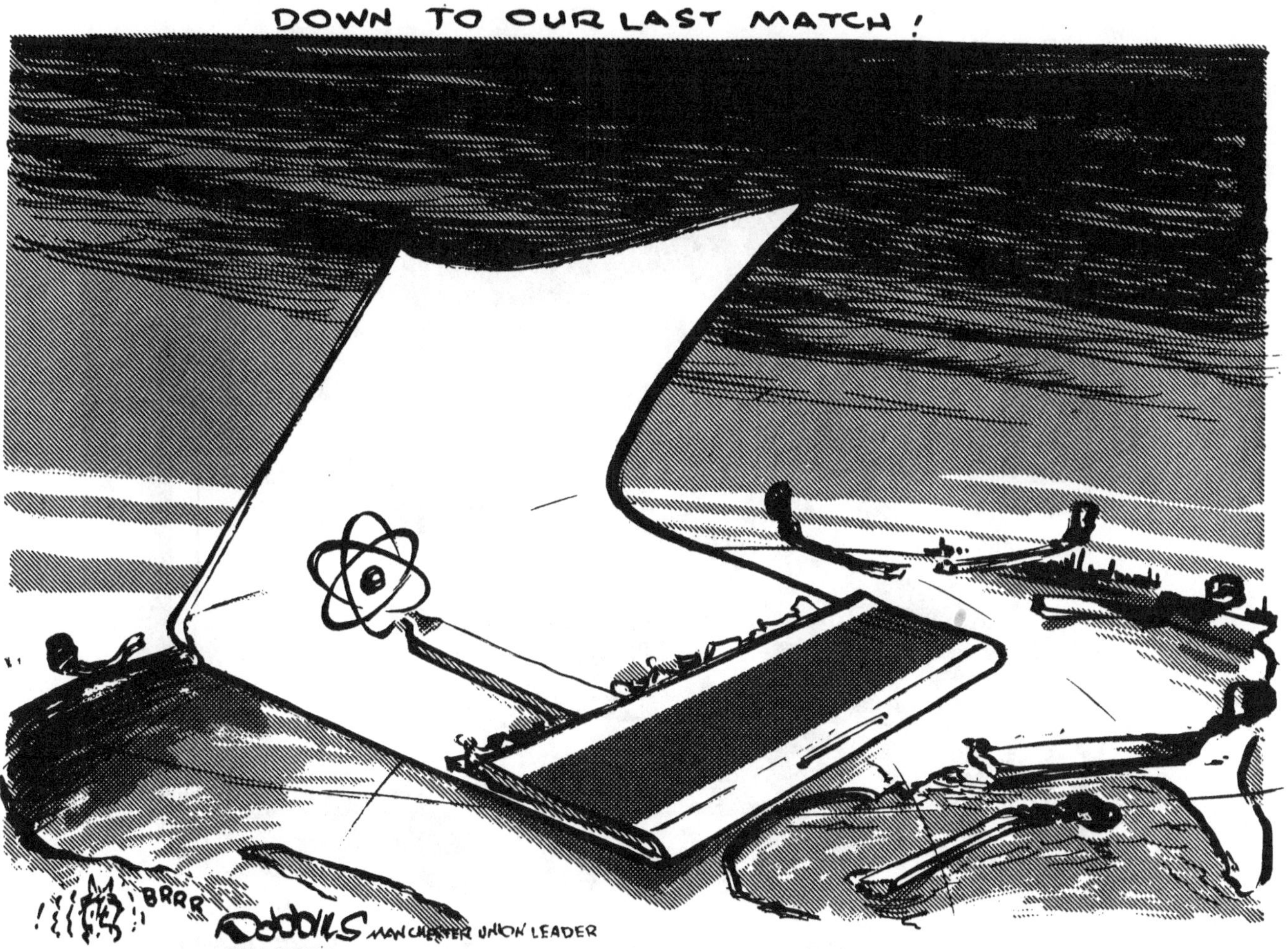
DOWN TO OUR LAST MATCH!
BRRR
DOBBINS MANCHESTER UNION LEADER

JIM DOBBINS
Courtesy Manchester Union-Leader

BOB BECKETT
Courtesy Burlington County
(N. J.) Times

JERRY FEARING
Courtesy St. Paul Dispatch

HY ROSEN
Courtesy Albany Times-Union

"YOU MAY BE UGLY MY SON, BUT YOU'RE ALL WE'VE GOT!"

Crime

Crime and terrorism continued unabated throughout the world during the year. Arson, for example, became the fastest growing crime in the United States, according to published governmental reports. It is also the costliest. It is believed that up to 19 percent of all fires and more than 40 percent of all fire insurance claims are the result of arson.

A special crime report released by the Ford Foundation in July emphasized an alarming spiral of violent crimes by teenagers. In fact, about 3 to 5 percent of those arrested account for more than half of the violent crimes committed by juveniles.

During the year Italy became the focal point of organized terrorist activities. A group calling itself the Red Brigades vowed to bring down the government by using kidnapping and other violent means. More than a score of victims were killed or wounded, the direct result of terrorist activities.

In early March the founders of the Red Brigades were brought to trial. With the trial less than a week old, the organization kidnapped Aldo Moro, the country's leading political figure, former premier, and president of the ruling Christian Democratic Party. Despite lengthy demands for ransom, the Italian government refused to negotiate for his release. Fifty-four days later his bullet-riddled body was found in an abandoned car in the center of Rome.

"...OIL?...NO, POT!"

BALDY
Courtesy Atlanta Constitution

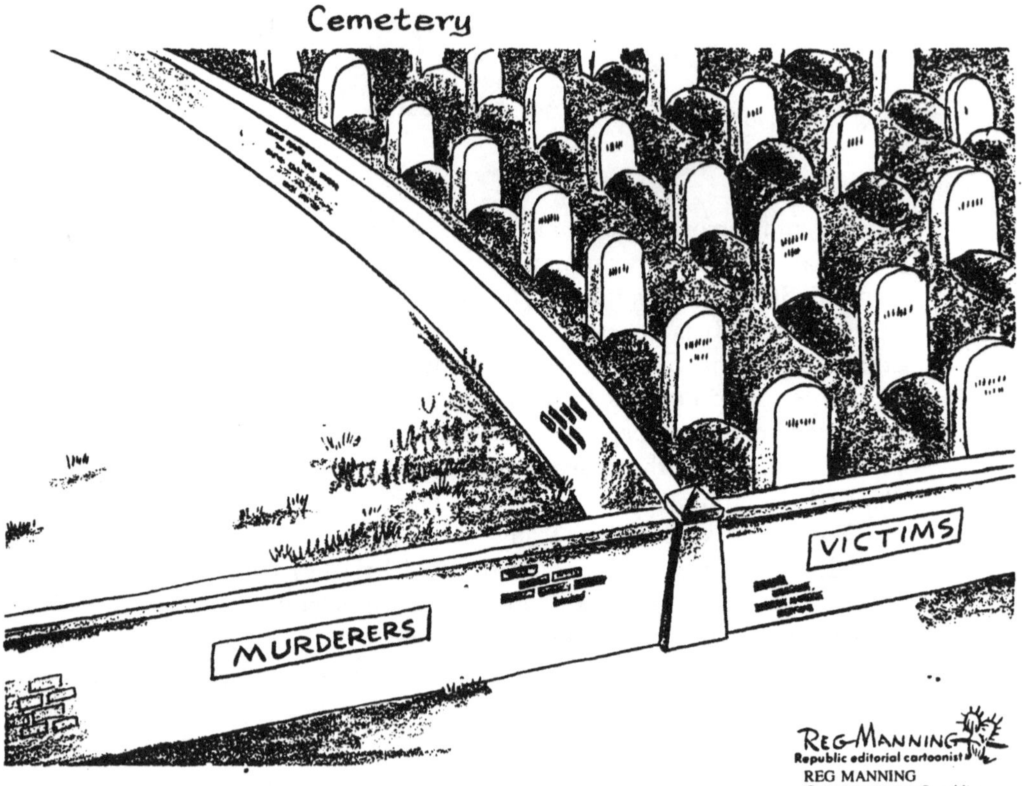
Cemetery
VICTIMS
MURDERERS
REG MANNING
Republic editorial cartoonist

REG MANNING
Courtesy Arizona Republic

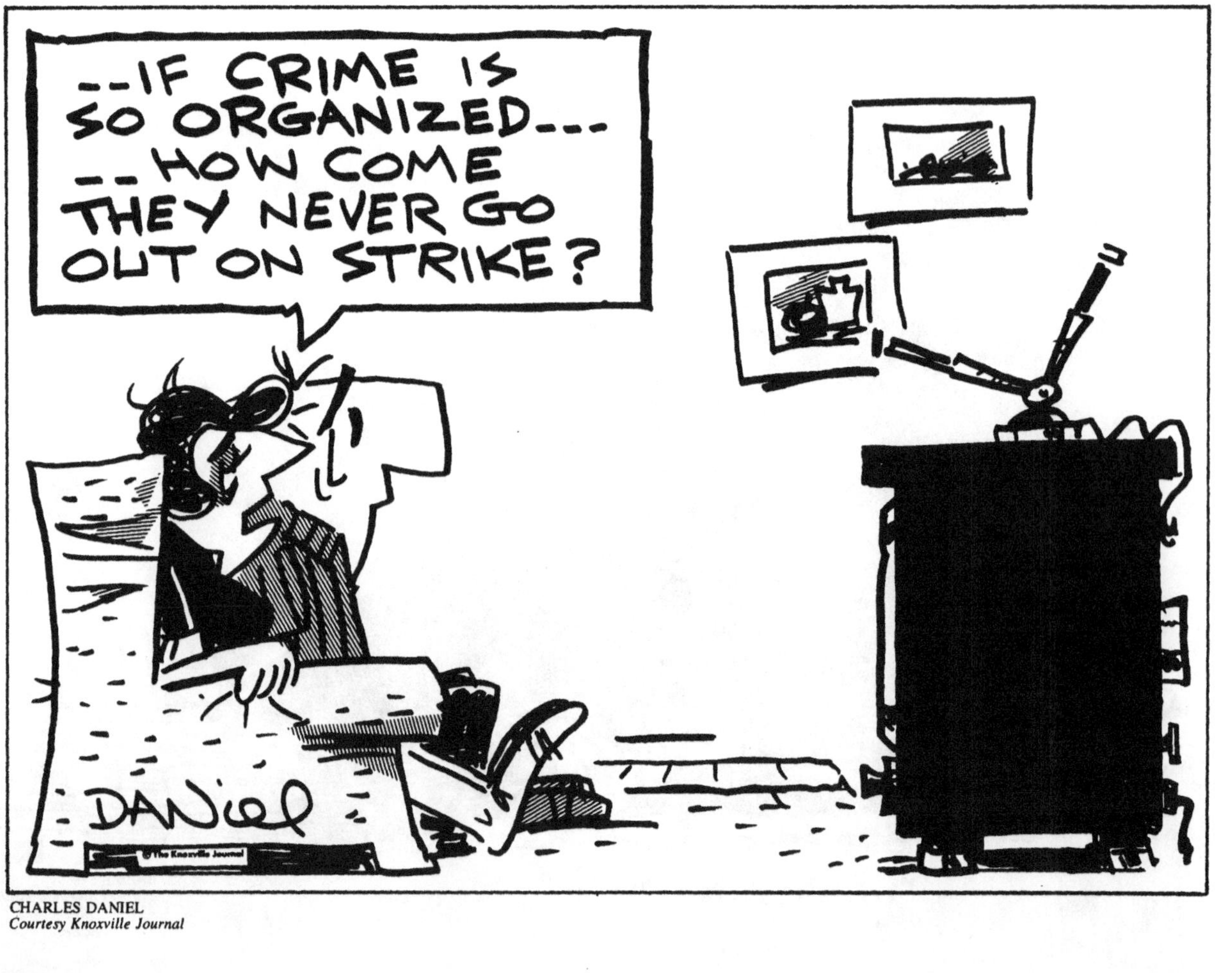
--IF CRIME IS SO ORGANIZED... ..HOW COME THEY NEVER GO OUT ON STRIKE?
DANIEL

CHARLES DANIEL
Courtesy Knoxville Journal

FRANK SPANGLER
Courtesy Montgomery (Ala.) Advertiser

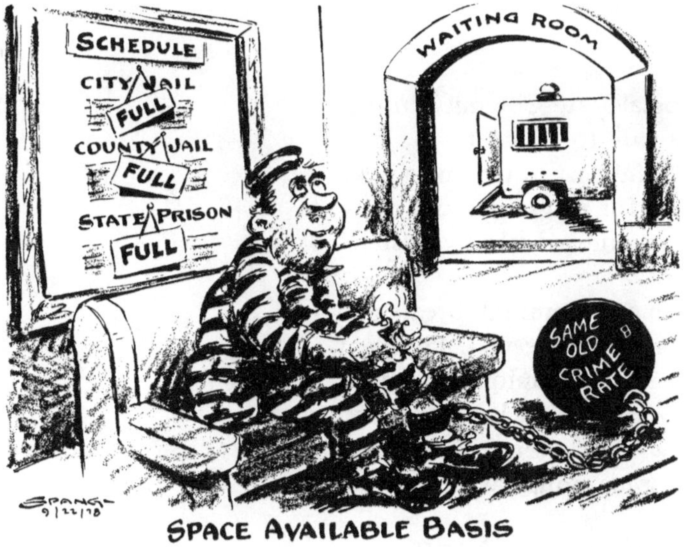
SCHEDULE
CITY JAIL
FULL
COUNTY JAIL
FULL
STATE PRISON
FULL
WAITING ROOM
SAME OLD CRIME RATE
SPACE AVAILABLE BASIS

SUFFER THE LITTLE CHILDREN

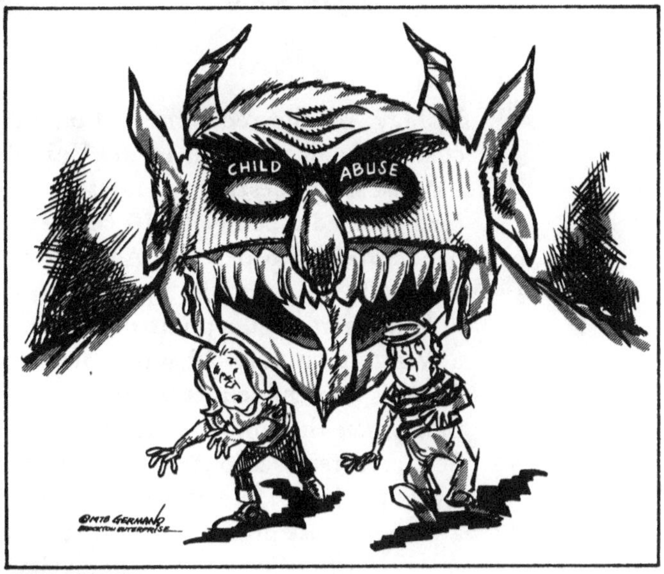
CHILD
ABUSE

EDDIE GERMANO
Courtesy Brockton Daily Enterprise

JOHN CRAWFORD
Courtesy Alabama Journal

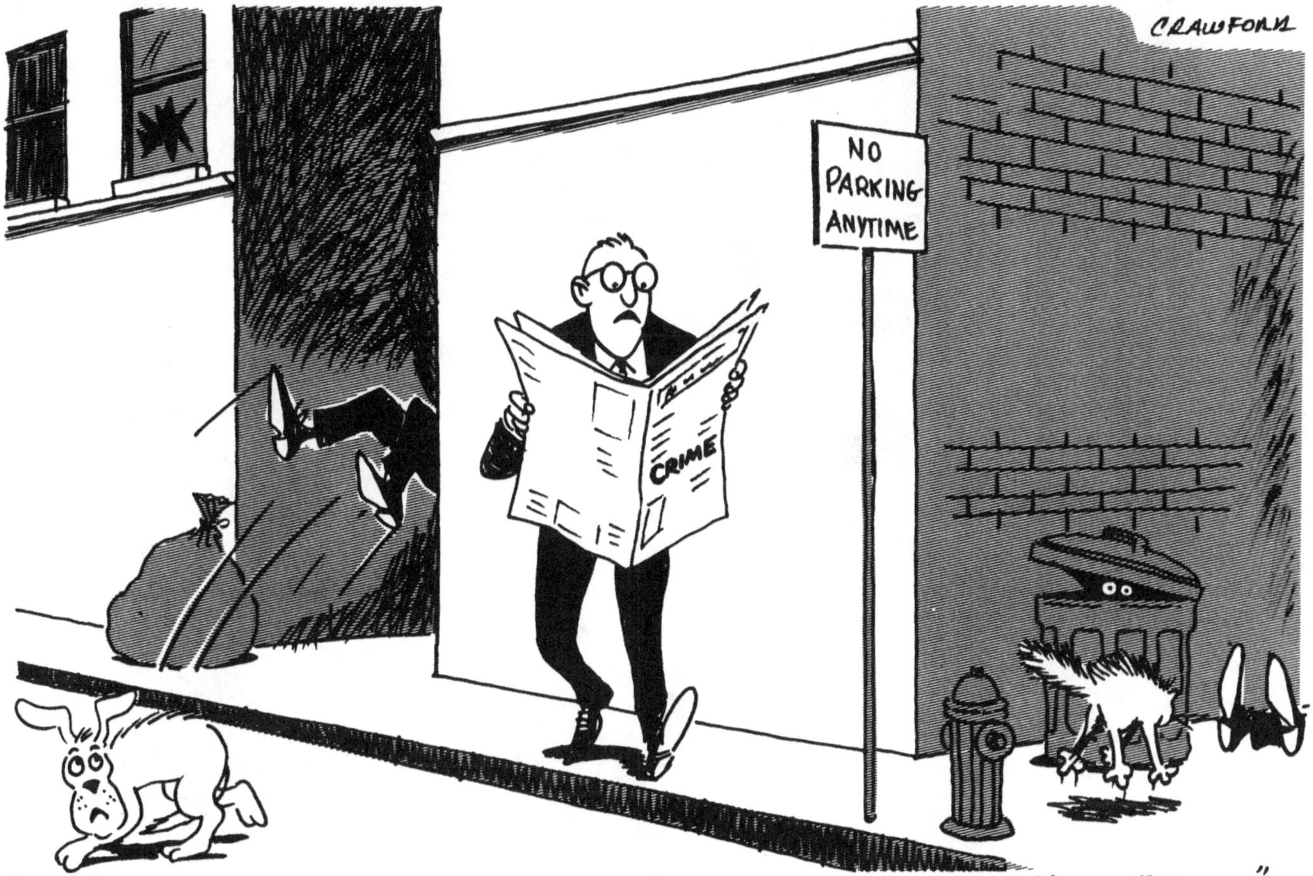
CRAWFORD
NO PARKING ANYTIME
CRIME
"HEY, JOE__ SAYS HERE OUR CHANCES OF BECOMING A CRIME VICTIM ARE INCREASING ---. JOE-- "

The Postal Service

In May, on the recommendation of the Postal Rate Commission, the cost of mailing a letter in the United States rose to 15 cents, the fifth increase in domestic mail rates in a decade. The cost of mailing a postcard jumped a penny to 10 cents, while rates for magazines and newspapers rose 29.6 percent. Advertising circulars and parcel rates also increased by 20.3 and 36.8 percent, respectively.

Wages remained a point of contention, with postal unions threatening a walkout on July 20 unless new wage demands were met. President Carter's wage guidelines became a central issue since the unions demanded more than the guidelines allowed. The issue was settled when the Postal Service offered a contract that seemed below the Carter ceiling. Postal workers, already one of the highest paid civil service groups, were awarded a 19.5 increase over the next three years.

The Post Office also abandoned its efforts to weaken a no-layoff clause that protects jobs against advances in technology.

CHUCK AYERS
Courtesy Akron Beacon Journal

'MAKE AN OFFER'

ED ASHLEY
Courtesy Toledo Blade

FRANCIS BRENNAN
©Newsweek

Collector's Item

JACK McLEOD
Courtesy Buffalo Evening News

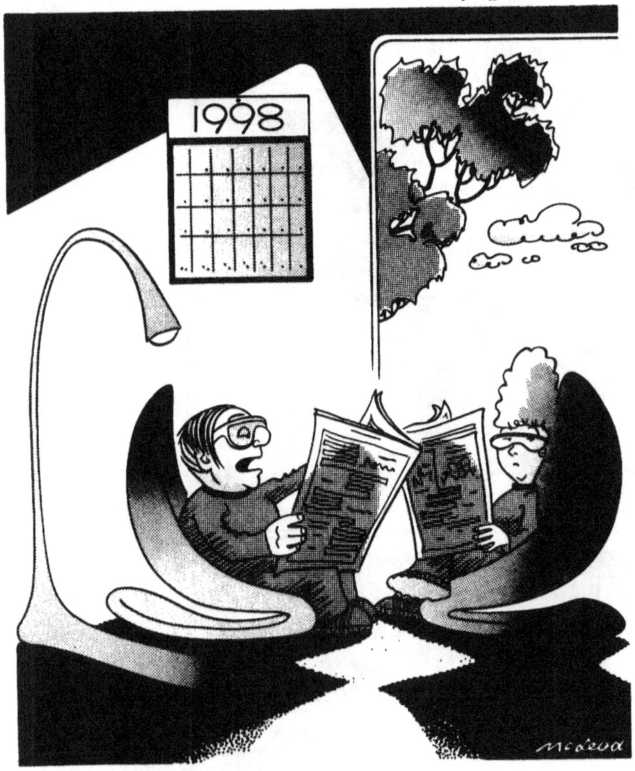
1998
McLEOD

'THE POSTAL RATE COMMISSION SAYS A 65¢ FIRST CLASS STAMP WILL DEFINITELY SOLVE THE DEFICIT THIS TIME'

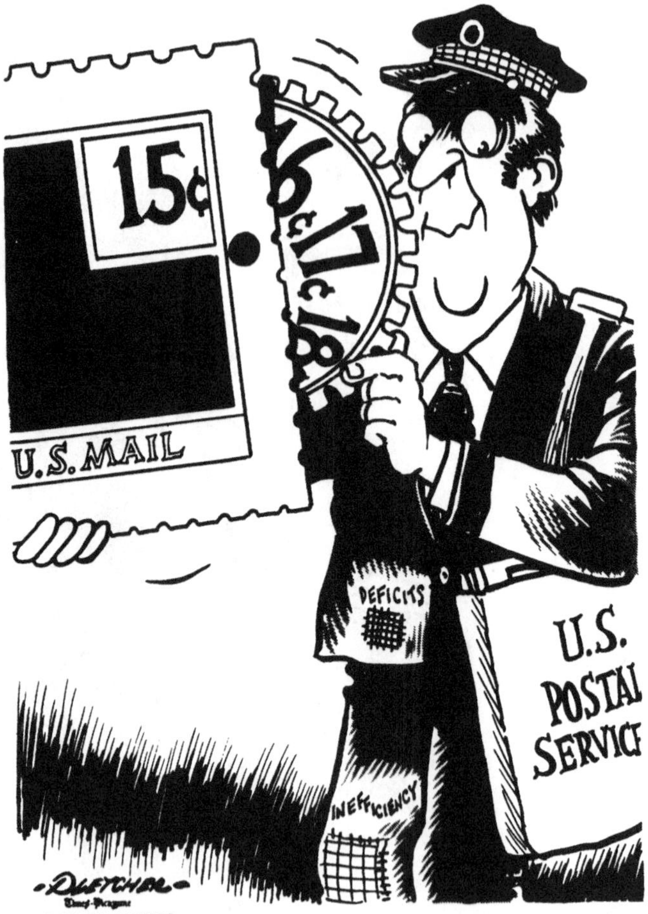
15¢
U.S. MAIL
16¢ 17¢ 18¢
DEFICITS
INEFFICIENCY
U.S. POSTAL SERVICE
PLETCHER

ELDON PLETCHER
New Orleans Times-Picayune
©Rothco

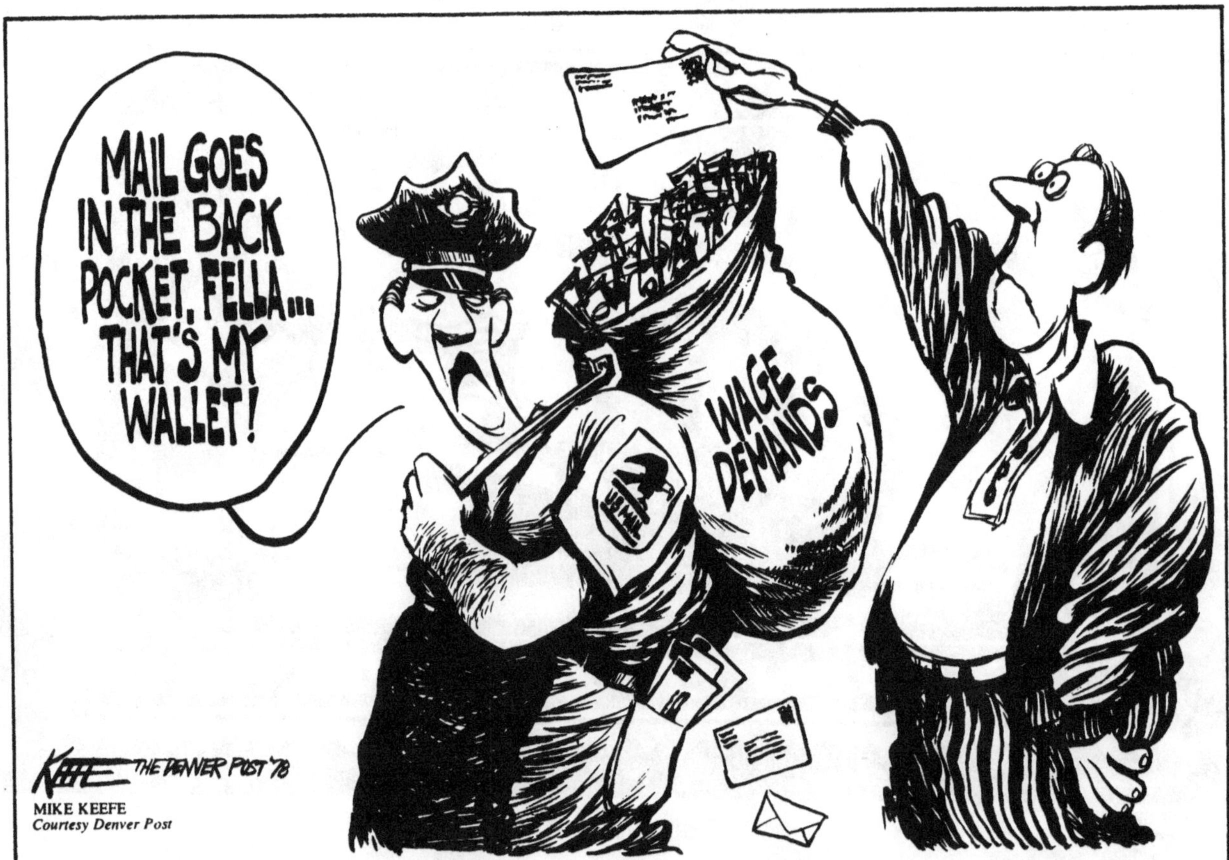
MAIL GOES IN THE BACK POCKET, FELLA... THAT'S MY WALLET!
WAGE DEMANDS
U.S. MAIL
KEEFE THE DENVER POST '78

MIKE KEEFE
Courtesy Denver Post

South of the Border

The Panama Canal became the focal point of one of the hottest political issues of 1978. Since 1903 the Panama Canal Treaty had governed American dealings in that area of the world. In 1978, however, congressional action significantly altered the traditional American stance in the Canal Zone.

The new treaty provides that Panama will assume complete control and ownership of the canal in 1999, but Panama also assumes jurisdiction in 1979. The U.S. will retain primary responsibility for defense of the canal until its transfer to Panama.

The Senate ratification vote was close, but President Carter's strong support for the new treaty carried the day.

Nicaragua became a center of turmoil during the year, with anti-government forces striving to overthrow the rule of strongman Anastasio Somoza. Left wing guerrillas stormed the National Palace and forced the government to give in to a long list of demands. Battles between guerrillas and the National Guard broke out in many key cities.

Guatemala and the Dominican Republic made attempts to reconcile the differences between the Somoza government and the guerrillas, but little success had been achieved by year's end.

JOHN TREVER
Courtesy Albuquerque Journal

It's a sedative that will allow them to operate later when they want to.

ALEJO VASQUEZ LIRA
Courtesy Excelsior (Mex.)

JOHN RIEDELL
Courtesy Peoria Journal

BILL DE ORE
Courtesy Dallas Morning News

DAN LYNCH
Courtesy Ft. Wayne Journal-Gazette

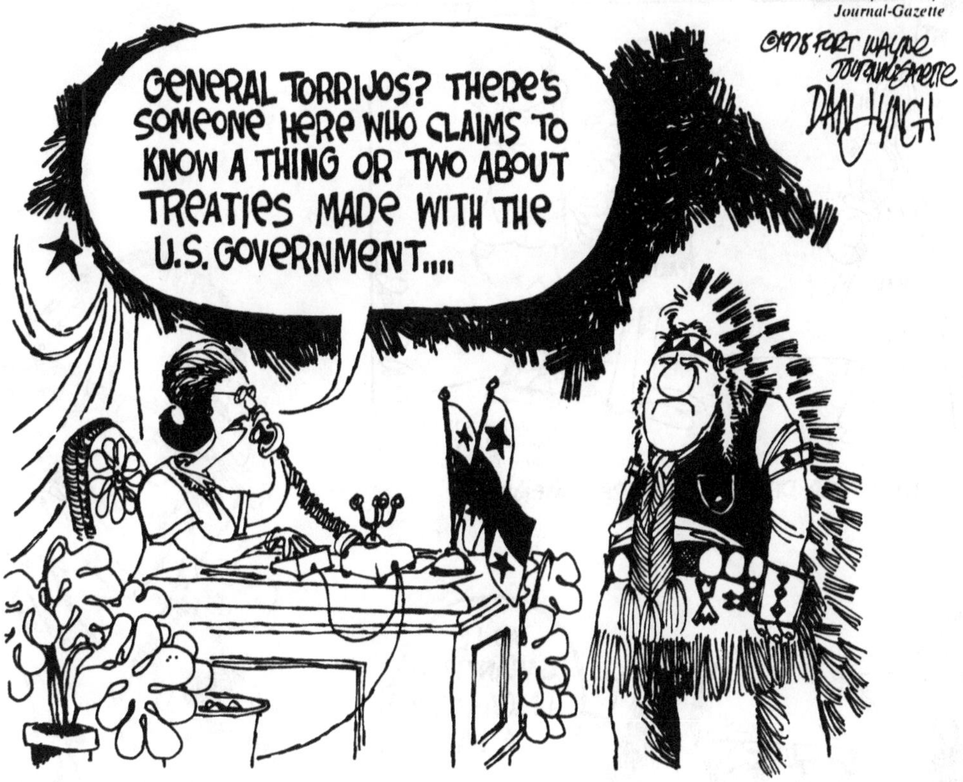
©1978 FORT WAYNE JOURNAL-GAZETTE
DAN LYNCH
GENERAL TORRIJOS? THERE'S SOMEONE HERE WHO CLAIMS TO KNOW A THING OR TWO ABOUT TREATIES MADE WITH THE U.S. GOVERNMENT....

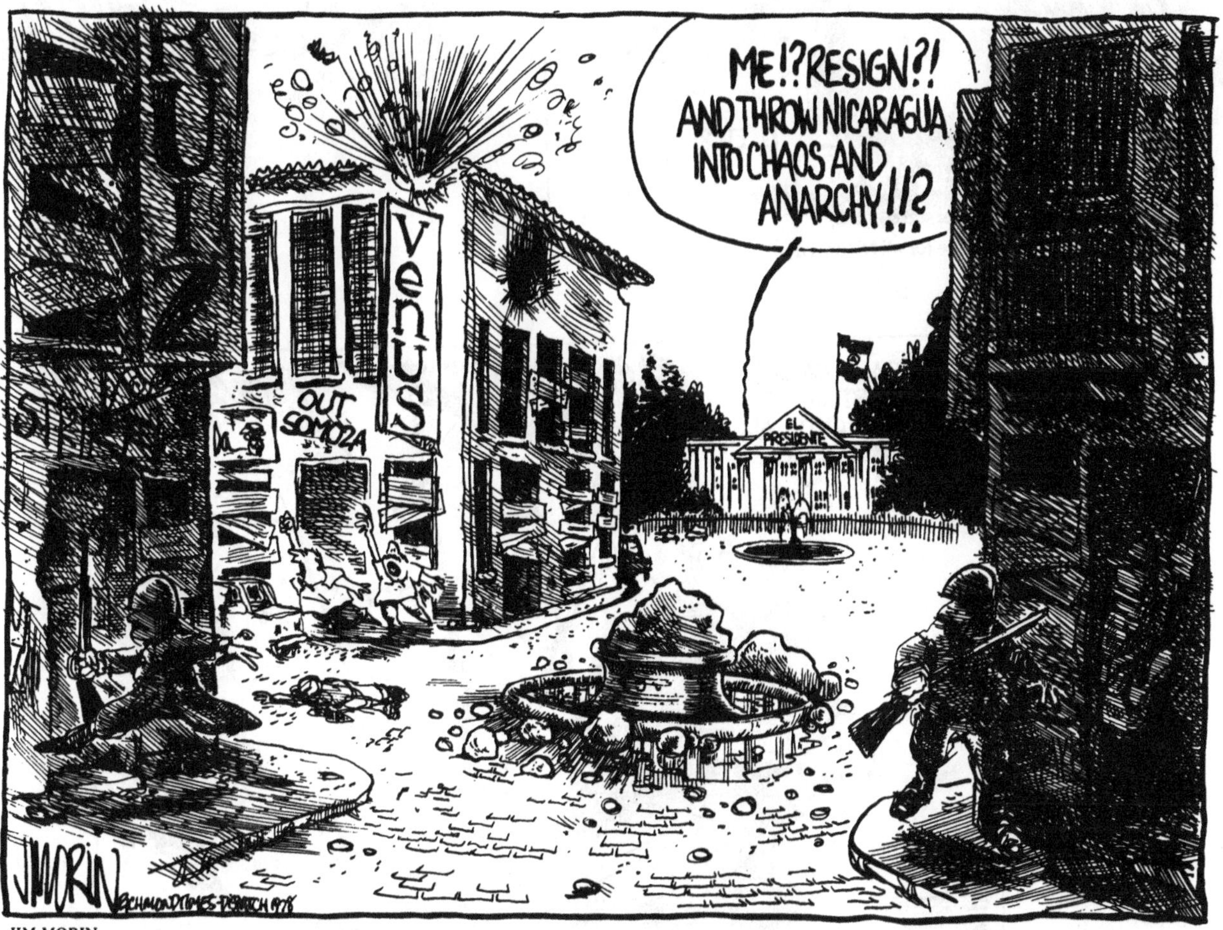
ME!?RESIGN?! AND THROW NICARAGUA INTO CHAOS AND ANARCHY!!?
VENUS
OUT SOMOZA
EL PRESIDENTE
J. MORIN
RICHMOND TIMES-DISPATCH 1978

JIM MORIN
Courtesy Richmond Times-Dispatch

"Opening or closing democracy in Panama?"

WILLIAM SOLANO
Courtesy La Nacion, San Jose, Costa Rica

¿APERTURA O APRETURA DEMOCRÁTICA PANAMEÑA?

WILLIAM SOLANO
Courtesy La Nacion, San Jose, Costa Rica

"I guarantee peace for all Nicaragua..."
-"...forever!"

NERO'S ENVY

HECTOR VALDES
Courtesy Villa Olympica

JOHN TREVER
Courtesy Albuquerque Journal

CHARLES WERNER
Courtesy Indianapolis Star

DENNIS RENAULT
Courtesy Sacramento Bee

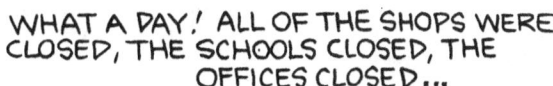

ETTA HULME
Courtesy Ft. Worth Star-Telegram

Test Tube Baby

The major medical news in 1978 was the birth, at 11:47 P.M. on July 25, of a baby conceived when British scientists united sperm and egg in a glass container. This was the first "test tube baby," and stirred controversy about the ethics of such experimentation.

Another medical controversy cropped up after the publication of a book, *In His Image: The Cloning of a Man*, by science writer David Rorvik. Cloning is reproduction using a cell from only one parent. The book alleged that such a cloning had actually taken place, but scientists remained skeptical.

Nevertheless, efforts in the field are continuing. In Great Britain, the day after the test tube baby, Louise Joy Brown, was born, surgeons operated on an infertile female and removed eggs for fertilization.

A second test tube baby was born during the year in a nursing home in Calcutta, India.

ED FISCHER
Courtesy Omaha World-Herald

MERLE TINGLEY
Courtesy London (Can.) Free Press

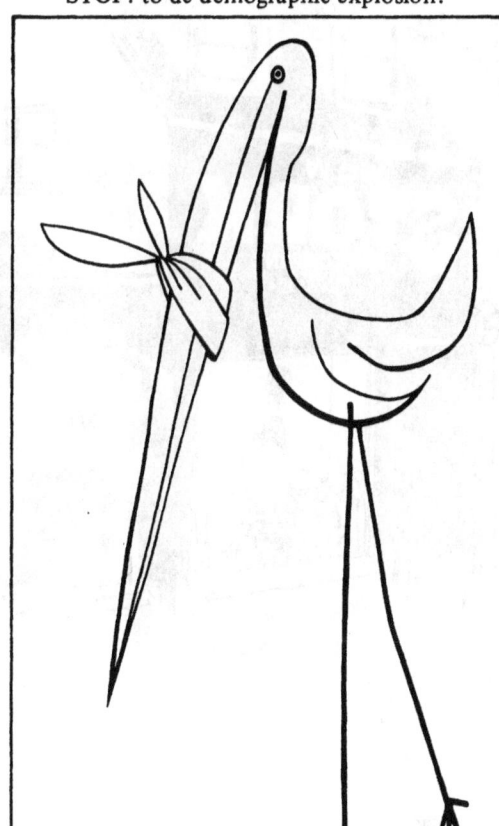

ALBERTO HUICI
Courtesy Jueves de Excelsior (Mex.)

DAVE GRANLUND
South Middlesex News
©Newspaper Enterprise Assn.

JIM LANGE
The Daily Oklahoman
©The Oklahoma Publishing Co.

DAN LYNCH
Courtesy Kansas City Times

WHAT HATH MAN WROUGHT?

LEW HARSH
Courtesy Scranton Times

DICK LOCHER
Courtesy Chicago Tribune

"First they said it was the stork, then stuff about birds and bees and your mommy's tummy ... and now ..."

VIC RUNTZ
Courtesy Bangor Daily News

ART BIMROSE
Courtesy Portland Oregonian

JACK JURDEN
Courtesy Wilmington Evening Journal-News

CHARLES DANIEL
Courtesy Knoxville Journal

Equal Rights Amendment

The Equal Rights Amendment stirred considerable controversy during the year, but failed to gain approval by any additional states. The proposed amendment to the U.S. Constitution, which would prohibit discrimination based on sex, has been ratified by 35 of the 38 states needed for the proposal to become law. In an apparently futile effort, four of the 35 states have rescinded previous action approving the amendment: Kentucky, Idaho, Nebraska, and Tennessee.

Some 50,000 supporters of ERA marched in Washington July 9 seeking an extension of the seven-year deadline for ratification as originally set by Congress. Under existing terms the period of ratification would have expired on March 22, 1979. On August 15, however, the House voted to extend the deadline for 39 months, and the Senate later approved the new date.

Proponents of the extension also defeated a proposal that would have allowed states to rescind approval during the extension period.

ETTA HULME
Courtesy Ft. Worth Star-Telegram

"DEAL YOU IN? YOU EXPECT US TO CHANGE RULES IN THE MIDDLE OF THE GAME?"

JEFF MACNELLY
Richmond News Leader
©Chicago Tribune—New York
News Syndicate

JOHN RIEDELL
Courtesy Peoria Journal

BERT WHITMAN
Courtesy Phoenix Gazette

Canada

Economic problems coupled with the Quebec separatist movement fueled unrest throughout Canada during the year. Prime Minister Pierre Trudeau announced severe cuts in government spending in an effort to strengthen business across the country.

Inflation continued to climb, unemployment remained high, and economic growth slowed. There was even controversy surrounding the Royal Canadian Mounted Police over the need to face official investigations nationally.

Canada's largest life insurance company, Sun Life Assurance Company of Canada, decided to transfer its headquarters from Montreal to Toronto. The decision was the result of strained relations between the Quebec business community and the Parti Quebecois government, which is dedicated to preserving French culture in Quebec and separating the province from the rest of Canada.

Officials of other large companies based in Montreal began to speak out about the Quebec business climate and the language issue. Many insisted that English is the language of their head offices and will remain so, no matter what the separatists demand.

JOHN COLLINS
Courtesy Montreal (Can.) Gazette

"HOW MANY PRACTICE SHOTS DO YOU GUYS NEED?"

ED ULUSCHAK
Courtesy Edmonton (Can.) Journal

JOHN COLLINS
Courtesy Montreal (Can.) Gazette

"DO YOU THINK I'VE LOST MY FORCE?"

VIC ROSCHKOV
Courtesy Toronto Star

CANADA

ANDY DONATO
Courtesy Toronto Sun

ROY CARLESS
Courtesy Canadian Transport

LEONARD NORRIS
Courtesy Vancouver (Can.) Sun

"I should warn you, officer . . . as a member of the government I tend to be above the law"

CAPITAL PUNISHMENT ANDY DONATO
Courtesy Toronto Sun

ANTHONY JENKINS
Courtesy Toronto Globe and Mail

ROY CARLESS
Courtesy Canadian Transport

"NO NEED TO PANIC, FOLKS! WE'RE MERELY STOPPING TO TAKE ON ICE!"

MERLE TINGLEY
Courtesy London (Can.) Free Press

VIC ROSCHKOV
Courtesy Toronto Star

JOHN COLLINS
Courtesy Montreal (Can.) Gazette

THE NEW WORD IS "ECONOMY" — PASS IT ON....

ROY CARLESS
Courtesy Canadian Transport

"HANG IN THERE! I'M OFF TO BORROW A PROP!"

The Environment

The U.S. Supreme Court decreed in June that the Endangered Species Act was to be given strict interpretation until Congress sees fit to give the law more precise language. The court also upheld a lower court ruling which suspended work on the nearly completed $116 million Tellico Dam on the Little Tennessee River. The court handed down its ruling to protect a tiny fish—the snail darter—from extinction. Later, however, the Tennessee Valley Authority announced the successful transfer of the snail darter to another river in Tennessee.

In the wake of the snail darter decision, Congress passed amendments to the Endangered Species Act to protect projects such as the Tellico Dam. In the future, similar projects can be evaluated and possibly exempted from certain provisions of the act.

The disposal of chemical wastes remained a growing problem. In August, people began moving away from an area near the abandoned Love Canal in Niagara Falls, New York after long-buried waste materials began bubbling to the surface. Drums in which the chemicals had been buried had rusted, thus allowing the waste matter to leak out.

KEN ALEXANDER
Courtesy San Francisco Examiner

"Just one snail darter in every river and America grinds to a halt!"

BILL DE ORE
Courtesy Dallas Morning News

ROGER HARVELL
*Courtesy Pine Bluff (Ark.)
Commercial*

BOB BECKETT
*Courtesy Burlington County
(N. J.) Times*

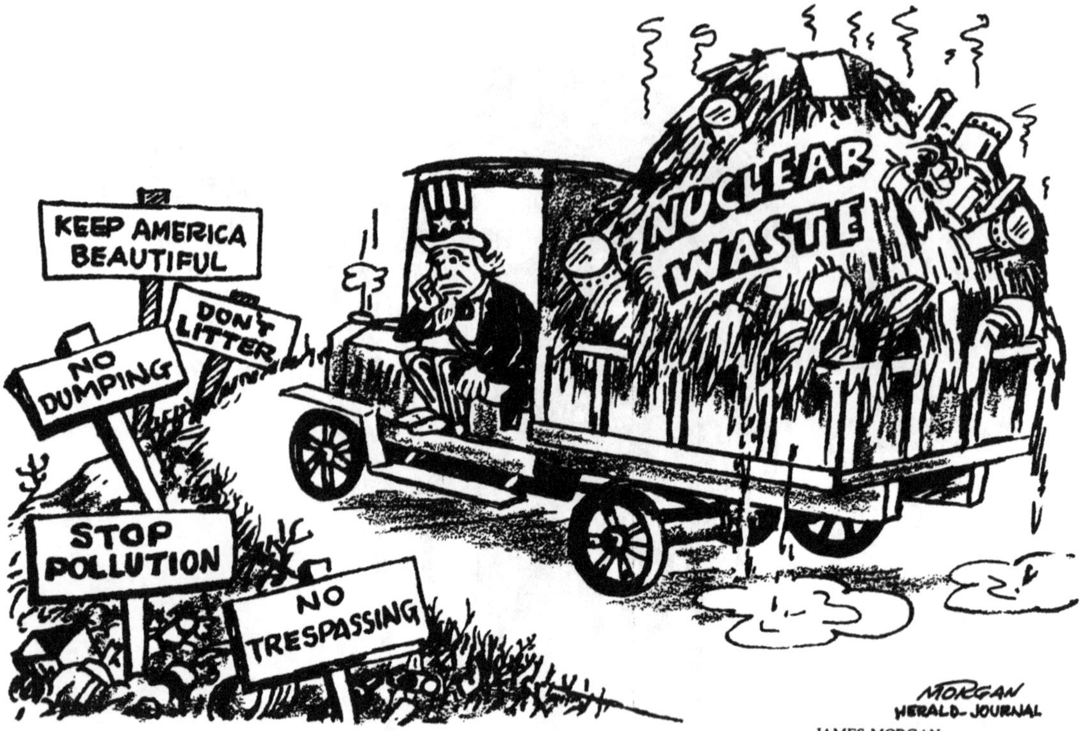
KEEP AMERICA BEAUTIFUL
DON'T LITTER
NO DUMPING
STOP POLLUTION
NO TRESPASSING
NUCLEAR WASTE
MORGAN
HERALD-JOURNAL

JAMES MORGAN
Courtesy Spartanburg Herald-Journal

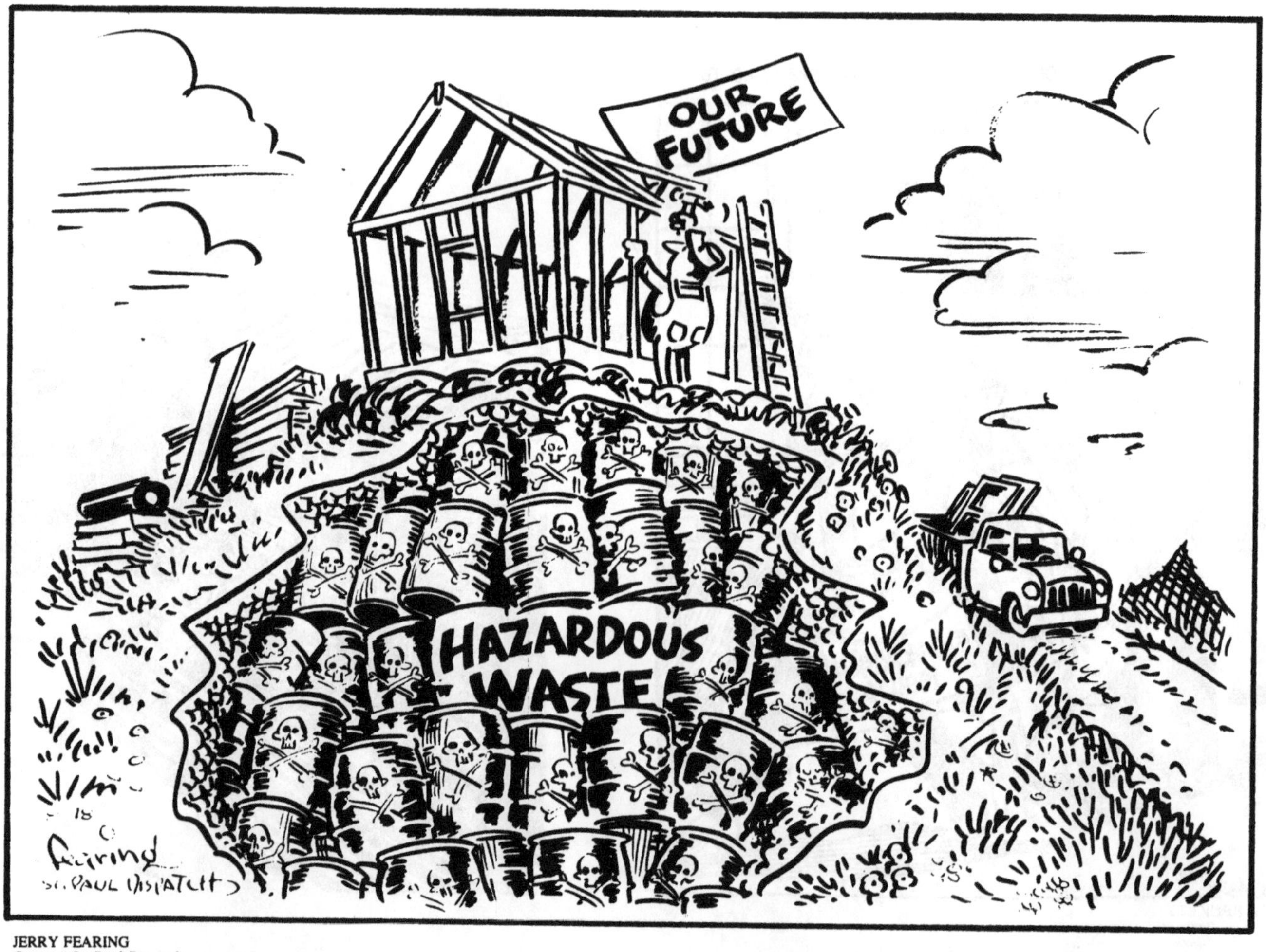
OUR FUTURE
HAZARDOUS WASTE
Fearing
ST. PAUL DISPATCH

JERRY FEARING
Courtesy St. Paul Dispatch

ART BIMROSE
Courtesy Portland Oregonian

ED STEIN
Courtesy Rocky Mountain News

"Faster! I think it's gaining on us!"

LARRY WRIGHT
Courtesy Detroit News

Choosing a Pope

The deaths of two popes within two months stunned Roman Catholics around the world. Pope Paul VI, after serving as pontiff since 1963, died on August 6. Although a social progressive, he had resisted pressures within the church for changes in traditional teaching on such issues as priestly celibacy, birth control, and the ordination of women.

On August 26 a new pope was elected—Cardinal Albino Luciani, patriarch of Venice, who assumed the name John Paul I. He served just over a month before suffering a fatal heart attack.

On October 16 a new pope waved to his followers in St. Peter's Square. He was Cardinal Karol Wojtyla of Poland, the first non-Italian pope in 455 years. He took the name John Paul II.

BOB ENGLEHART
Courtesy Dayton Journal Herald

MIKE KEEFE
Courtesy Denver Post

TERRY MOSHER (AISLIN)
Courtesy Montreal Gazette

LARRY WRIGHT
Courtesy Detroit News

DANA SUMMERS
Courtesy Fayetteville
(N. C.) Times

Obituaries

Some of the world's most famous figures in politics and entertainment departed from the scene in 1978.

Hubert H. Humphrey, 66, U.S. senator from Minnesota and often referred to as "Mr. Democrat," died January 13 in Waverly, Minnesota. Humphrey had aggressively espoused liberal causes throughout his career, which brought him to within an eyelash of the presidency in 1968.

The entertainment world lost one of its all-time great comedians, Charlie Chaplin, who passed away in Switzerland at the age of 88. Chaplin perfected his "Little Tramp" character in silent films and worked as an actor, writer, director, and producer in the modern era.

Charles Boyer, one of the great screen lovers of the 1930s and 1940s, committed suicide two days after the death of his wife. Ventriloquist Edgar Bergen, who made Charlie McCarthy and Mortimer Snerd household names, died at the age of 75.

Norman Rockwell, the artist who many believe captured small town America better than anyone else, died on November 8 at age 84. He had painted more than 350 covers for *The Saturday Evening Post*.

CHARLES BROOKS
Courtesy Birmingham (Ala.) News

HUGH HAYNIE
Louisville Courier-Journal
©Los Angeles Times Syndicate

STEVE GREENBERG
*Courtesy Valley News,
Van Nuys, Cal.*

So short the reign; so long the shadow

MOMMA

KATE PALMER
Courtesy Greenville (S.C.) News

JOHN BRANCH
Courtesy Chapel Hill News

JERRY FEARING
Courtesy St. Paul Dispatch

JON KENNEDY
Courtesy Arkansas Democrat

The loved one

'One of my favorite nephews...always trying to improve your old uncle...'

GUERNSEY LEPELLEY
Courtesy Christian Science Monitor

. . . And Other Issues

ED FISCHER
Courtesy Omaha World-Herald

BOB ENGLEHART
Courtesy Dayton Journal Herald

TERRY MOSHER (AISLIN)
Courtesy Montreal Gazette

BOB ALEXANDER
Courtesy Lawrence (Mass.) Eagle-Tribune

EDDIE GERMANO
Courtesy Brockton Daily Enterprise

And In The Land Of Lincoln

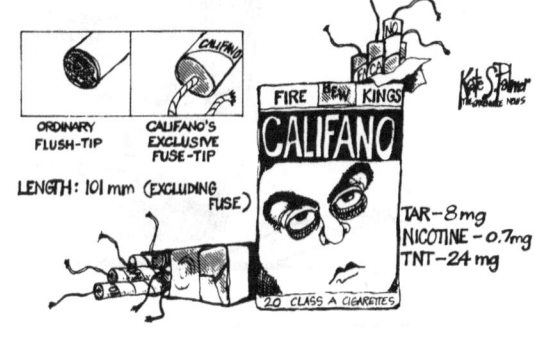

KATE PALMER
Courtesy Greenville (S.C.) News

LARRY WRIGHT
Courtesy Detroit News

BILL DAY
Courtesy Oakland Press

TIM MENEES
Courtesy Pittsburgh Post-Gazette

DOUG SNEYD
©Sneyd Syndicate

JOHN BRANCH
Courtesy Chapel Hill News

DICK WALLMEYER
Long Beach Press-Telegram
©Register and Tribune Syndicate

LEONARD NORRIS
Courtesy Vancouver (Can.) Sun

"I first noticed it right after they put those new-fangled scanners in the supermarket checkout . . ."

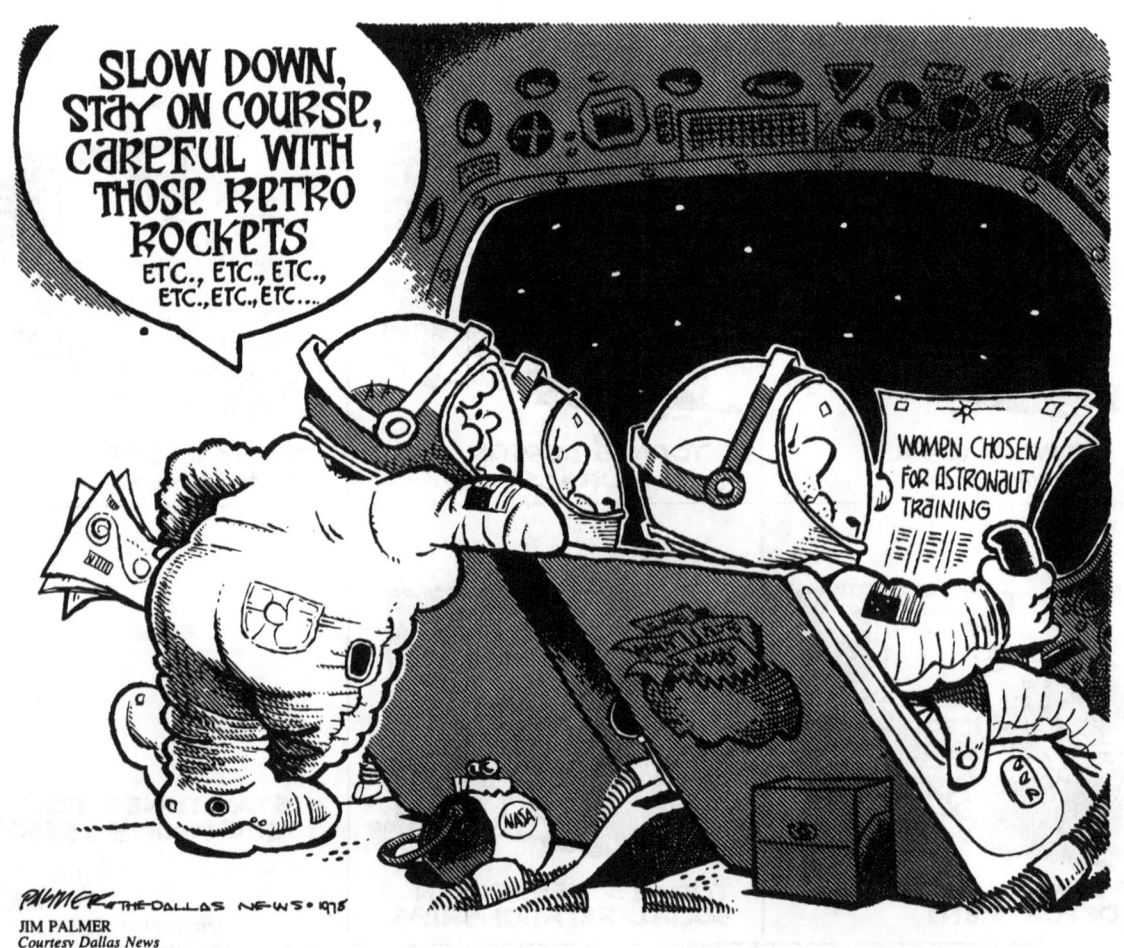

JIM PALMER
Courtesy Dallas News

BRIAN BASSET
Courtesy Seattle Times

BALDY
Courtesy Atlanta Constitution

FRANK SPANGLER
Courtesy Montgomery (Ala.) Advertiser

KEN ALEXANDER
Courtesy San Francisco Examiner

Past Award Winners

PULITZER PRIZE EDITORIAL CARTOON

1922—Rollin Kirby, New York World
1924—J. N. Darling, New York Herald Tribune
1925—Rollin Kirby, New York World
1926—D. R. Fitzpatrick, St. Louis Post-Dispatch
1927—Nelson Harding, Brooklyn Eagle
1928—Nelson Harding, Brooklyn Eagle
1929—Rollin Kirby, New York World
1930—Charles Macauley, Brooklyn Eagle
1931—Edmund Duffy, Baltimore Sun
1932—John T. McCutcheon, Chicago Tribune
1933—H. M. Talburt, Washington Daily News
1934—Edmund Duffy, Baltimore Sun
1935—Ross A. Lewis, Milwaukee Journal
1937—C. D. Batchelor, New York Daily News
1938—Vaughn Shoemaker, Chicago Daily News
1939—Charles G. Werner, Daily Oklahoman
1940—Edmund Duffy, Baltimore Sun
1941—Jacob Burck, Chicago Times
1942—Herbert L. Block, Newspaper Enterprise Association
1943—Jay N. Darling, New York Herald Tribune
1944—Clifford K. Berryman, Washington Star
1945—Bill Mauldin, United Feature Syndicate
1946—Bruce Russell, Los Angeles Times
1947—Vaughn Shoemaker, Chicago Daily News
1948—Reuben L. (Rube) Goldberg, New York Sun
1949—Lute Pease, Newark Evening News
1950—James T. Berryman, Washington Star
1951—Reginald W. Manning, Arizona Republic
1952—Fred L. Packer, New York Mirror
1953—Edward D. Kuekes, Cleveland Plain Dealer
1954—Herbert L. Block, Washington Post
1955—Daniel R. Fitzpatrick, St. Louis Post-Dispatch
1956—Robert York, Louisville Times
1957—Tom Little, Nashville Tennessean
1958—Bruce M. Shanks, Buffalo Evening News
1959—Bill Mauldin, St. Louis Post-Dispatch
1961—Carey Orr, Chicago Tribune
1962—Edmund S. Valtman, Hartford Times
1963—Frank Miller, Des Moines Register
1964—Paul Conrad, Denver Post
1966—Don Wright, Miami News
1967—Patrick B. Oliphant, Denver Post
1968—Eugene Gray Payne, Charlotte Observer
1969—John Fischetti, Chicago Daily News
1970—Thomas F. Darcy, Newsday
1971—Paul Conrad, Los Angeles Times
1972—Jeffrey K. MacNelly, Richmond News Leader
1974—Paul Szep, Boston Globe
1975—Garry Trudeau, Universal Press Syndicate
1976—Tony Auth, Philadelphia Enquirer
1977—Paul Szep, Boston Globe
1978—Jeff MacNelly, Richmond News Leader

NOTE: Pulitzer Prize Award was not given 1923, 1936, 1960, 1965, and 1973.

NATIONAL HEADLINERS CLUB AWARDS EDITORIAL CARTOON

1938—C. D. Batchelor, New York Daily News
1939—John Knott, Dallas News
1940—Herbert Block, Newspaper Enterprise Association
1941—Charles H. Sykes, Philadelphia Evening Ledger
1942—Jerry Doyle, Philadelphia Record
1943—Vaughn Shoemaker, Chicago Daily News
1944—Roy Justus, Sioux City Journal
1945—F. O. Alexander, Philadelphia Bulletin
1946—Hank Barrow, Associated Press
1947—Cy Hungerford, Pittsburgh Post-Gazette
1948—Tom Little, Nashville Tennessean
1949—Bruce Russell, Los Angeles Times
1950—Dorman Smith, Newspaper Enterprise Association
1951—C. G. Werner, Indianapolis Star
1952—John Fischetti, Newspaper Enterprise Association
1953—James T. Berryman and Gib Crockett, Washington Star
1954—Scott Long, Minneapolis Tribune
1955—Leo Thiele, Los Angeles Mirror-News
1956—John Milt Morris, Associated Press
1957—Frank Miller, Des Moines Register

PAST AWARD WINNERS

1958—Burris Jenkins, Jr., New York Journal-American
1959—Karl Hubenthal, Los Angeles Examiner
1960—Don Hesse, St. Louis Globe-Democrat
1961—L. D. Warren, Cincinnati Enquirer
1962—Franklin Morse, Los Angeles Mirror
1963—Charles Bissell, Nashville Tennessean
1964—Lou Grant, Oakland Tribune
1965—Merle R. Tingley, London (Ont.) Free Press
1966—Hugh Haynie, Louisville Courier-Journal
1967—Jim Berry, Newspaper Enterprise Association
1968—Warren King, New York News
1969—Larry Barton, Toledo Blade
1970—Bill Crawford, Newspaper Enterprise Association
1971—Ray Osrin, Cleveland Plain Dealer
1972—Jacob Burck, Chicago Sun-Times
1973—Ranan Lurie, New York Times
1974—Tom Darcy, Newsday
1975—Bill Sanders, Milwaukee Journal
1976—No award given
1977—Paul Szep, Boston Globe
1978—Dwane Powell, Raleigh News and Observer

THOMAS NAST AWARD

1978—Jeff MacNelly, Richmond News Leader

NATIONAL NEWSPAPER AWARD/CANADA

1949—Jack Boothe, Toronto Globe and Mail
1950—James G. Reidford, Montreal Star
1951—Len Norris, Vancouver Sun
1952—Robert La Palme, Le Devoir, Montreal
1953—Robert W. Chambers, Halifax Chronicle-Herald
1954—John Collins, Montreal Gazette
1955—Merle R. Tingley, London Free Press
1956—James G. Reidford, Toronto Globe and Mail
1957—James G. Reidford, Toronto Globe and Mail
1958—Raoul Hunter, Le Soleil, Quebec
1959—Duncan Macpherson, Toronto Star
1960—Duncan Macpherson, Toronto Star
1961—Ed McNally, Montreal Star
1962—Duncan Macpherson, Toronto Star
1963—Jan Kamienski, Winnipeg Tribune
1964—Ed McNally, Montreal Star
1965—Duncan Macpherson, Toronto Star
1966—Robert W. Chambers, Halifax Chronicle-Herald
1967—Raoul Hunter, Le Soleil, Quebec
1968—Roy Peterson, Vancouver Sun
1969—Edward Uluschak, Edmonton Journal
1970—Duncan Macpherson, Toronto Daily Star
1971—Yardley Jones, Toronto Sun
1972—Duncan Macpherson, Toronto Star
1973—John Collins, Montreal Gazette
1974—Blaine, Hamilton Spectator
1975—Roy Peterson, Vancouver Sun
1976—Andy Donato, Toronto Sun
1977—Terry Mosher, Montreal Gazette

Index

Aguila, Dani, 69
Alexander, Bob, 85, 152
Alexander, Ken, 19, 141, 156
Artley, Bob, 51, 83
Ashley, Ed, 59, 106, 124
Atseff, Timothy, 31, 104
Ayers, Chuck, 69, 90, 123

Baldowski, Cliff (Baldy), 24, 98, 121, 156
Barnett, Jerry, 46, 74, 101
Basset, Brian, 23, 93, 156
Basset, Gene, 43, 76, 77, 94
Beckett, Bob, 119, 142
Bender, Jack, 25
Berry, Jim, 18, 83, 85, 102
Bimrose, Art, 21, 134, 144
Bissell, Charles, 83, 86, 96, 116
Bissell, Phil, 106
Borgman, Jim, 21, 30, 47, 87
Borgstedt, Douglas, 37, 66, 92
Branch, John, 18, 149, 154
Brennan, Francis, 52, 124
Brooks, Charles, 24, 68, 100, 147

Campbell, Sandy, 27, 52, 65
Cantone, Vic, 22, 114
Carless, Roy, 138, 139, 140
Collins, John, 137, 138, 140
Commodore, Chester, 76, 102
Craig, Eugene, 22, 38, 62
Crawford, John, 41, 74, 122
Curtis, Tom, 17, 26, 50, 76

Daniel, Charles, 55, 121, 134
Day, Bill, 106, 153
Dean, Pap, 41
De Ore, Bill, 113, 127, 142
Dobbins, Jim, 28, 46, 118
Donato, Andy, 37, 138, 139
Doyle, Jerry, 109, 116
Drebelbis, Robert, 99

Engelhardt, Tom, 73, 84, 86
Englehart, Bob, 106, 145, 151
Erickson, Lou, 28, 107

Evers, Frank, 21, 54, 63, 113

Fearing, Jerry, 119, 143, 149
Fischer, Ed, 93, 112, 131, 151
Fisher, George, 39, 83, 93, 110
Flannery, Tom, 60, 105, 111

Gamble, Ed, 65, 78, 91
Garner, Bill, 34, 49, 88, 116
Germano, Eddie, 20, 122, 152
Gold, Jack, 117
Graham, Bill, 51, 87, 103
Granlund, Dave, 29, 132
Grant, Lou, 25, 47, 100, 109
Greenberg, Steve, 41, 148

Harsh, Lew, 99, 104, 133
Harvell, Roger, 95, 142
Haynie, Hugh, 43, 71, 72, 148
Henrikson, Art, 61, 71
Hill, Draper, 25, 109, 117
Hubenthal, Karl, 36, 45, 58, 104
Huici, Alberto, 132
Hulme, Etta, 75, 79, 130, 135

Interlandi, Frank, 27, 36, 92

Jenkins, Anthony, 34, 139
Jurden, Jack, 30, 50, 134

Keefe, Mike, 61, 125, 146
Kennedy, Jon, 21, 84, 150
Konopacki, Michael, 27

Lange, Jim, 59, 132
Lanigan, Jack, 40
Lawlor, Rob, 27, 37, 110
LePelley, Gurnsey, 30, 69, 79, 150
Levine, David, 16
Locher, Dick, 19, 53, 97, 133
Long, Scott, 71, 92, 118
Lynch, Dan, 74, 128, 133

MacIntosh, Craig, 33, 70, 81
MacNelly, Jeff, 11, 12, 35, 82, 115, 136

INDEX

McLeod, Jack, 40, 105, 125
McVey, Kevin, 56

Manning, Reg, 65, 73, 121
Margulies, Jimmy, 39, 105
Menees, Tim, 96, 153
Miller, David W., 38
Morgan, Jim, 143
Morin, Jim, 32, 94, 117, 128
Morris, John Milt, 51
Mosher, Terry (Aislin), 14, 146, 152

Norris, Leonard, 139, 155

Osrin, Ray, 48, 65, 89, 102

Palmer, Jim, 48, 107, 155
Palmer, Kate, 29, 148, 152
Peterson, Clyde, 21, 84, 86
Pierotti, John, 18, 62
Pletcher, Eldon, 50, 57, 125
Powell, Dwane, 13, 33, 53, 78

Rajski, R. B., 100
Rawls, S. C., 39, 73, 113
Renault, Dennis, 36, 79, 130
Riedell, John, 127, 136
Robinson, Jerry, 44, 47, 70, 114
Roschkov, Vic, 42, 138, 140
Rosen, Hy, 60, 108, 112, 119
Runtz, Vic, 103, 134

Sack, Stephen, 58, 90
Shevchik, John, 56
Sneyd, Doug, 44, 68, 153
Solano, W., 129
Spangler, Frank, 122, 156
Stampone, John, 57, 100
Stein, Ed, 80, 144
Sullivan, Robert, 54, 75, 91
Summers, Dana, 40, 63, 146
Szep, Paul, 26, 46, 48, 107

Taylor, Bob, 34, 42, 110
Taylor, Mark, 92, 103
Thompson, Vern, 62, 66, 73, 80
Tingley, Merle, 61, 132, 139
Trever, John, 88, 126, 129

Uluschak, Edd, 43, 64, 114, 138

Valdes, Hector, 116, 129
Valtman, Ed, 23, 35, 87, 99
Vasquez Lira, Alejo, 127

Wallmeyer, Dick, 82, 85, 95, 154
Wells, Clyde, 64, 67, 98
Werner, Chuck, 21, 37, 57, 130
Whitman, Bert, 73, 95, 136
Wood, Art, 52, 56
Wright, Dick, 31, 83, 98
Wright, Larry, 144, 146, 152

www.ingramcontent.com/pod-product-compliance
Lightning Source LLC
Chambersburg PA
CBHW080547170426
43195CB00016B/2707